RKO CLASSIC SCREENPLAYS

What Price Hollywood?

Directed by George Cukor
Screenplay by: Gene Fowler
and
Rowland Brown

An Andrew Velez Book

FREDERICK UNGAR PUBLISHING CO.
New York

INTRODUCTION

David O. Selznick, the legendary producer of *What Price Hollywood?* and production head of RKO in 1932, believed the whole world wanted to know what went on in Hollywood. That his evaluation about Hollywood was accurate is borne out by the endless stream of films through the decades since. Among the more memorable are Billy Wilder's *Sunset Boulevard* (1950), Gene Kelly and Stanley Donen's *Singin' in the Rain* (1952), Clifford Odets's *The Big Knife* (1955), and Blake Edwards's recent *S.O.B.* (1981).

Selznick's film is still one of the most effective glimpses into behind-the-scenes filmmaking ever committed to celluloid. It represents George Cukor's first major directorial effort as well, and served as the forerunner of the three versions of *A Star Is Born* (1937, 1954, 1976). Cukor also served as director of the 1954 version, which starred Judy Garland and James Mason.

Although 1932 was a disastrous year financially for RKO, as well as other studios, it was also significant in marking a commitment by RKO under Selznick's aegis to make better and first-rate films. Merian C. Cooper (*King Kong*), Fred Astaire, Katharine Hepburn, and George Cukor all signed contracts with the studio. One of the year's few moneymakers, *A Bill of Divorcement*, in which Hepburn made her film debut, was the beginning of her long professional association and friendship with Cukor. (In 1933 Hepburn won her first Oscar for her performance in *Morning Glory*, directed by Lowell Sherman. As an actor, Sherman turned in a bravura performance as the dipsomaniacal director in *What Price Hollywood?*)

Written by Jane Murfin and Ben Markson, (with an "assist" from Gene Fowler and Rowland Brown), the screenplay of *What Price Hollywood?* was based on a story by Adela Rogers St. John. Originally titled *The Truth About Hollywood*, (another working title was *Hollywood Merry-Go-Round*), the film was intended to be a comeback vehicle for the "It" girl of the 1920s, Clara Bow, whose career had been ruined by scandal and ill health. The central role eventually went to Constance Bennett. The rise of Mary Evans is traced from her obscurity as a Brown Derby waitress to movie stardom. She is befriended by Max Carey (Lowell Sherman), a brilliant, alcoholic director who guides her career to success.

(Sherman's performance may in part have been inspired from experiences with his then brother-in-law, John Barrymore. Sherman was known to have suffered his own bouts with drinking as well.) After she becomes a star, Bennett meets and marries a polo-playing millionaire (Neil Hamilton). Their marriage founders under the pressures of her stardom. Ultimately they are reunited after the suicide of her friend and mentor.

In the 1937 version of *A Star Is Born*, the characters of the director and the husband were merged into a single one, and the poignant juxtaposition of rising and falling stars was repeated in the remakes as well. Gregory Ratoff played Julius Saxe, a movie mogul modeled not a little after Selznick himself. Within the structure of his now classic tale is reflected a vision of a sybaritic world of parvenues, sycophants, and hangers-on prone to lavish lifestyles and the values of movie-fan magazines.

Even as the nation remained deeply in the throes of the Great Depression, Hollywood continued to turn out films in quantity for a public that would become ever more eager to escape the all too harsh realities of daily life. The star-studded Oscar-winning film of 1932 was M-G-M's *Grand Hotel*. Mae West made her screen debut in *Night After Night* opposite George Raft, and Johnny Weissmuller appeared for the first time as Tarzan. Other memorable films of the year were *Scarface* with Paul Muni, Garbo in *Mata Hari*, *A Farewell to Arms* with Gary Cooper and Helen Hayes, *Back Street, I Am a Fugitive From a Chain Gang, Red Dust* with Gable and Jean Harlow, and Marlene Dietrich in Josef von Sternberg's exotic *Shanghai Express*.

What was to become known as "the Golden Age of Hollywood," the 1930s, saw the production of a variety and a richness in films never to be matched or repeated. The studio system that made them is long gone, as is the audience for which the world's largest movie theatre, the Radio City Music Hall, was opened in December 1932. After more than fifty-two years, and whatever the changes in our lives since then (real and apparent), the modern fairy tale of the unknown girl who yearns to be a famous star and gets her wish, at a price, is still powerful. The land of klieg lights and lotuses, of outsized emotions and egos, of scandal and tragedy, continues to compel our attention with all the invisible power of which dreams are made.

Andrew Velez

CAST:

Mary Evans	Constance Bennett
Max Carey	Lowell Sherman
Lonny Borden	Neil Hamilton
Julius Sax	Gregory Ratoff
Muto	Brooks Benedict
The Maid	Louise Beavers

CREDITS:

Written by	Gene Fowler
	Rowland Brown
Based on a Story by	Adela Rogers St. John
Screenplay by	Jane Murfin
	Ben Markson
Executive Producer	David O. Selznick
Director	George Cukor
Associate Producer	Pandro S. Berman
Photographed by	Charles Rosher
Art Director	Carroll Clark
Costumes Supervised by	Margaret Pemberton

WHAT PRICE HOLLYWOOD?

Adapted from an Original Story

by

Adela Rogers St. Johns

FADE IN

For main title and exposure of credits, there is a background of carousel music. The series of quick dissolves shows trick shots of each of the principal characters in the story. It is as though they are riding a gigantic merry-go-round. Double-exposures show a background formed by various Hollywood places, photographic studies of Hollywood. In the foreground is each character riding on a merry-go-round animal. The only character not *on a horse, camel, etc., is the girl, Mary Evans. She, too, is on the Hollywood Merry-Go-Round, but she is riding in a Cinderella pumpkin coach, with two rats for horses.*

Sound—carousel music (some established tune that keeps the mood of the picture, such as "I'm Forever Blowing Bubbles")

(Note: If desired, the name of each character may be used superimposed on the scene depicting the persons pertinent to the play; thus introducing them)

LAP DISSOLVE OUT

LAP DISSOLVE IN

SERIES OF DISSOLVES
A birds-eye view (taken from Goodyear blimp) of Hollywood.
Double expose against this birds-eye view the following:
A *A testimonial advertisement for silk stockings. A large picture*
of a beautiful pair of silk-clad legs. A vignette of a star's face—
printed testimonial:
"For real beauty, there's nothing like SHEER SILK"
(Facsimilie script) "MIGNON LEE"
B *A Fashion Page:*
(Printed)
"What the Stars are wearing. Jean Summers shows her new
wardrobe for Spring."
There follows a view of a girl wearing a smart street dress.
Double expose a figure, in smart teddy, donning a street dress
almost exactly like the one on the Fashion Page. The page turns...
C *An advertisement for lipstick. A large picture of the lower half*
of a girl's face, with lips pursed—applying lipstick—then the
caption—
(Printed)
"Hollywood's Favorite Lips
Renee Dupont uses KISS ME
Lip Rouge."
Sound—During the progress of foregoing lap dissolves there is a
phonograph playing the same tune as has been heard at beginning
of screen credit dissolves.
The phonograph sound carries over the next dissolve and through
part of scene

LAP DISSOLVE OUT

LAP DISSOLVE IN

INTERIOR MARY'S ROOM—DAY
Pull back from lipstick and lips to full shot of Mary Evans, who is
putting lipstick on before mirror. She is in a modish but inexpen-

sive ensemble that is in accord with the garb of the motion picture stars depicted in magazine.
Sound—the phonograph is still playing

LAP DISSOLVE

INTERIOR MARY'S ROOM—DAY
Another angle—Mary is at the dressing table, completing her toilette. On the dresser is the fan magazine, lying open. She looks down at it and turns a page. Registers delight. She cuts the picture (Clark Gable) from the magazine and gazes admiringly at it.
Sound—the phonograph is still playing

CUT TO INTERIOR MARY'S ROOM—DAY
Close up Mary's mirror. Pictures of various well known stars are pasted on mirror, the camera pans to show quick flashes of each picture. The picture which Mary now pastes (or possibly pins to draperies behind mirror) is definitely that of Clark Gable. The camera pulls back showing Mary ready to leave. The phonograph runs down as Mary is picking up hat. She goes over to turn phonograph motor off. Then she plays a scene to Gable's photograph.
MARY: *(playing scene to Gable's photo—in a decided Garbo voice and manner)* Goodbye, Darlink. I luff you. I luff you, my poor darlink. Oh, how I mees you—*(she switches suddenly from the Garbo voice and manner as she finishes the sentence)*—you great big, handsome lug! *(decidedly tough; she goes out of door with a grand manner)*

INTERIOR HALLWAY OF MARY'S APARTMENT—DAY
Moving shot—We follow Mary along hall. As she walks she is stopped by a grandly dressed gentleman of middle-age. He is clad in silk topper, morning coat and gardenia, striped trousers, etc. He is carrying a small make-up box. He looks like a bored banker.
MAN: Oh, Miss Evans, would you lend me a quarter? I haven't got the carfare out to Universal.
MARY: Got a job, eh? What'll the landlord think? *(she fumbles in her purse)*

3

MAN: I'm getting ten bucks for a bit. But the director said it was a part that'll stand out.

MARY: *(gives him the quarter)* Don't forget the little girl that gave you a start.

LAP DISSOLVE

EXTERIOR HOLLYWOOD BOULEVARD STORE—DAY
Mary walks down street, camera following her. She stops before a store window, where there is a wax model, modernistic, on which is a gorgeous evening gown. As she looks at it, there is a dissolve showing Mary herself (as though in a dream) in the same gown that is on the model. Suddenly a man comes behind her (in the dream) and begins to raise her dress as though to remove it. Mary's face registers consternation. She is aroused from her dream and we see a man in the store-window, taking the dress from the mannequin, leaving it nude. Mary, roused from her dream, walks out of scene, a bit deflated.

CUT TO EXTERIOR HOLLYWOOD BOULEVARD, GRAUMAN'S CHINESE—DAY
Long shot—Mary comes into lobby of theater. There are signs of activity. Carpets are being laid, a cluster of sun-arc lights are being rolled across the lobby. A big sign says:

> *GALA OPENING*
> *TONIGHT*
> *WORLD PREMIERE OF*
> *ALICE DURANT'S GREATEST PICTURE*
> *"SECRET LOVE"*
> *SEE THE STARS IN PERSON*

Mary stops before a large easel on which a poster bears the picture of Alice Durant in the arms of the leading man. As Mary stands there, a dissolve shows her own face taking the place of that of Alice. A theater attendant moves the easel to let a sun-arc past and the face dissolves back to that of Alice. Mary drops her purse and looks down as she stoops to recover purse.

CUT TO EXTERIOR CHINESE THEATER—DAY
Close shot—As Mary is recovering purse, she sees she is standing on one of the cement blocks in the lobby of the Chinese Theater. The footprints of Norma Talmadge (or who have you) are in the particular block where Mary is standing. The name of the star is written there. We see Mary step into the impressions of the Talmadge (or what have you) prints. A dissolve shows the Talmadge name fading and the name "Mary Evans" written there. Then we see a janitor's floorbrush strike against her feet. The feet move, and as the brush moves across the prints, we see it rub out the prints and the name "Mary Evans."

LAP DISSOLVE

EXTERIOR BROWN DERBY—LATE AFTERNOON
As Mary comes into the shot, an old woman holds out some gardenias for her to buy. She moves in.

CUT TO INTERIOR BROWN DERBY—LATE AFTERNOON
Trucking shot—Mary walks grandly into the place. She passes the salad and cold-cut counter, at which stands a dark-complexioned, sheikish employee. He looks like Ramon Navarro and seems out of place in his employment.
MARY: *(in passing)* Hello, cold cuts.
She hurries on—passes a booth where two movie executives are sitting.
FIRST EXECUTIVE: Women like dark complected men.
SECOND EXECUTIVE: It's a good part. I think you're right, the Latin types are coming back. Remember what I told...
His voice trails as Mary passes. She goes by a table at which two men and a woman are sitting.
SECOND MAN: *(at a table halfway toward kitchen to his companions, bragging)* And was I drunk, and was she beautiful? Well, the next day I...

5

His voice also trails off amid laughter as Mary passes. She keeps walking, passes another man at telephone. He is excited and apparently is bargaining. He is an insipid fellow.

THIRD MAN: Why should I take less? I'm worth twenty-five hundred a week of anybody's money. I got a name, I'm box office. You ought to know...

His voice also trails as Mary comes to booth where Muto is sitting by himself. Muto gives her the eye. Nick is standing by Muto. This part of the set is near the kitchen door. Nick looks at Mary with disapproval.

NICK: *(to Mary)* What's the matter with your watch?

MARY: I've got an electric clock and forgot to pay the bill.

NICK: Maybe you're too good for this job? *(he walks away)*

MARY: *(calling after him)* Listen, you heel, are you that dumb you don't know I'm sticking here—*(gives him the big Garbo business)*—because I got a great beeg love for you? *(she goes into the kitchen. Muto takes in the scene.)*

LAP DISSOLVE TO INTERIOR BROWN DERBY—EARLY EVENING

Mary comes out of kitchen door, backwards. She is carrying a tray on which there are many sugar bowls. She puts tray down on a serving table and then takes a full bowl of sugar to Muto's table. She pays no attention to him as she replaces the empty sugar bowl on Muto's table with the full one. He reaches over and takes her hand. She looks at him with restrained disgust.

MUTO: Listen, Sugar. Do you want to go in pictures? I just wrote a great part for a girl like you.

MARY: *(takes her hand away)* Why don't you stick to blackmailing?

MUTO: *(he is sore—threateningly)* Want me to call Nick over?

MARY: Sure. Call him over and tell about that seventeen-year-old girl you put in pictures. *(Muto is perturbed)* And I'll call your editor and tell him he's got a keyhole-peeper and a blackmailer for a columnist. *(She goes to table where two dear old ladies are sitting)*

ONE OLD LADY: *(sizes Mary up with approval—to Mary)* What a beautiful girl! Why aren't *you* in the movies, dear?

MARY: That's what I wonder myself.

SECOND OLD LADY: You're the prettiest girl we've seen.
MARY: *(to second old lady)* That's awfully sweet of you. You'll see me in pictures some day.
FIRST OLD LADY: Our brother owns a theater back in Muncie, Indiana. His name's James McGuire. Ever hear about him?
MARY: Sure. Who hasn't?
They smile as she goes out of the scene.

CUT TO INTERIOR BROWN DERBY—EARLY EVENING
Third man, as in Scene 10. He's closing his telephone conversation. Mary stands beside him to take order.
THIRD MAN: *(over telephone)* That's my price. I just got through making a personal appearance tour over the Palsy-Walsy Circuit and I'm box office. I got box-office sticking out all over me. So long. *(he hangs up and looks up at Mary)* Well, what you got?
MARY: I got box office, too.
THIRD MAN: *(who has no sense of humor)* I want some cold cuts.
MARY: A lot of *ham?*

CUT TO INTERIOR BROWN DERBY—EARLY EVENING
Second man, as in Scene 10. He is still bragging. He is a homely, loud-mouthed fellow.
SECOND MAN: *(to his companions, bragging)* And was she beautiful and was I drunk?
Mary looks at the sugar-bowl and finds it is almost full, so she passes on.

CUT TO INTERIOR BROWN DERBY—EARLY EVENING
First executive, as in Scene 10. They are still talking shop. One executive is writing on tablecloth. A closeup of tablecloth shows a column of figures.
FIRST EXECUTIVE: Women are getting fed up with blonde types.
SECOND EXECUTIVE: Like I said, the Latin types are coming back. *(Mary is putting sugar into the bowl)* Look at Clark Gable. He's through. The Latin types...
His voice trails as Mary goes toward salad counter. She stops to put down her sugar tray.

7

CUT TO INTERIOR BROWN DERBY—EARLY EVENING
Mary and the Salad Man.

MARY: An order of cold cuts for Mr. Box Office. *(confidential)* Listen, the Latin types are coming back. I just heard that—*(she nods off)*—big producer cracking to his yes-man.
COLD CUTS: What did I tell you? *(he is holding a big salami and gestures with it)* You can fool some of the people all the time, but you can't never fool the American women. They want the sophisticated love.
MARY: I'll take a good old-fashioned cowboy.

CUT TO EXTERIOR BROWN DERBY RESTAURANT— EVENING
Carey and Gardenia Woman. Carey drives up in his Rolls Royce town car. His man, James, hands him from the car. Mr. Carey is rather slopped. The Gardenia Woman holds out her wares.
GARDENIA WOMAN: Will you have a gardenia for your buttonhole, Mr. Carey?
CAREY: I'll buy them all.
WOMAN: All of them?
CAREY: Yes, mother. *(brings out handful of bills)* I'll control the gardenia market. Then nobody else will have any and I'll get all the girls. *(gives her the money)* Here you are.
WOMAN: You don't need gardenias to get girls, Mr. Carey.
CAREY: Just for that I'm going to send you home in my car.
WOMAN: Oh, Mr. Carey...
CAREY: *(to James)* Take her home, James. *(He hands her into car, meanwhile holding box of gardenias under one arm—he kisses her hand as he leans into car and says goodbye)*
WOMAN: *(as they start off)* Thanks so much, Mr. Carey. Don't forget me in your next picture... I'd be another Marie Dressler.

CUT TO INTERIOR BROWN DERBY—EVENING
Trucking shot—Carey with gardenia box under arm. As he passes booths and tables, he imitates flower girl tossing his blossoms. When he gets to table occupied by Executives of Scenes 10 and 14, he seems to be tired. Executives leaving table are being helped into

coats by Nick. All the while during Carey's gardenia march, there is a succession of greetings, to each of which he replies with "What's new?"

INCIDENTAL: Hello, Carey? Going to a funeral? Good evening, Mr. Carey!

As Carey reaches table which is being deserted by movie executives, Carey collides with a mannishly dressed woman, who is on her way out. She gives him a dirty look.

CAREY: *(to mannish woman)* I'm sorry, sir. *(She gives him a glare and moves out of scene. He looks after her, holding a gardenia towards her, off)* Who'll buy my violets?

CUT TO INTERIOR BROWN DERBY RESTAURANT— NIGHT

Carey and Nick. Nick motions for Carey to sit at table where Movie Executives have been drinking.

NICK: Congratulations, Mr. Carey!

CAREY: For what?

NICK: *(indulgently)* For the fine picture they're opening tonight. *(claps hands for waitress)*

Carey sits down. Looks at figures written on tablecloth.

CUT TO INTERIOR BROWN DERBY RESTAURANT— NIGHT

Mary and another waitress. They are filling glasses with water. Mary nudges the waitress.

MARY: There's Carey! In one of your booths. Let me wait on him, will you? I gave you Wallace Beery last week.

WAITRESS: Okay, but how much bonus do I get?

MARY: You can have the tip. I'm looking for a break. *(pauses)* And I'm going to get it. *(she moves off to Carey)*

CUT TO INTERIOR BROWN DERBY—NIGHT

Muto. He looks off at Carey. Is interested. Gets up.

CUT TO INTERIOR BROWN DERBY—NIGHT

Mary is starting to change tablecloth on Carey's table.

9

CAREY: *(he has a pencil. Looking at column of figures)* Just a minute. Last tablecloth I ate on was ten thousand dollars short. Bring me six glasses of water. Six separate glasses.

MARY: Going to put out a fire?

CAREY: I said six glasses.

MARY: And how many pots of coffee?

> *Muto enters scene. Carey pays no attention to him. Muto sits down.*

CAREY: *(to Mary)* One pot of black coffee. And six glasses of water. *(to Muto, whom Carey evidently dislikes, pointedly, as though Muto were still standing)* Won't you have a seat?

> *Mary goes out of scene.*

MUTO: How about giving me a full page ad for the new picture, Carey?

CAREY: Every hour you're out of jail you're away from home.

MUTO: Somebody's been knocking me to you. What you got against me?

CAREY: Your parents for one thing. They should have known better. Every time I read that column of yours, I burn up. Am I keeping you from going some place?

MUTO: You got me all wrong. I'm only trying to get along. *(Mary enters with a tray bearing a pot of coffee, cup and saucer, silver, napkin and six glasses of water. She puts them on the table. He ogles her.)* Hello, sugar!

> *Mary ignores his greeting.*

CAREY: *(he takes each glass of water as it is handed him and puts gardenias in the glasses—to Mary)* Here! *(he pushes one glass with gardenias toward her)* Take this to those dear old ladies. *(looks off)*

MARY: Can you spare it? *(she takes glass and gardenia and moves off)*

MUTO: I hear you got a wow of a picture.

CAREY: I bet they count the silver every time you eat here.

CUT TO INTERIOR BROWN DERBY—NIGHT
Same two old ladies of Scene 11.

MARY *(setting glass down with gardenias)* Mr. Carey—*(nodding off)*— sent this to you.

FIRST OLD LADY: *(looking off, nodding and smiling; to her companion)* Myra, it's the man I said resembled Brother Jim.

SECOND OLD LADY: *(to Mary)* How thoughtful! Who is he, dear?

10

MARY: Maximilian Carey, the great director. His picture, "Secret Love," opens tonight at Grauman's Chinese.
FIRST OLD LADY: I wonder if he could put us in one of his pictures?

CUT TO INTERIOR BROWN DERBY—NIGHT
CAREY: *(calling off)* Miss! Oh, Miss! Bring me a telephone. *(to Muto)* Seeing you reminded me of something unpleasant. Thanks.
MUTO: *(rises and moves out)* If that's the way you feel.

CUT TO INTERIOR BROWN DERBY—NIGHT
Mary brings telephone and plugs it in. Carey is trying to manage his coffee, but is shaking and having difficulty.
MARY: What you need is a couple of straws.
CAREY: That's a good idea. Bring me the straws that broke the camel's back. *(into telephone)* Gladstone 1025. *(to Mary)* What's a pretty girl like you doing in a place like this?
MARY: I'm just studying human nature.
CAREY *(he gets his number—Mary stands by)* Hello! That you, sweetheart? Believe it or not, you can't guess where I'm at. What's that? You don't give a what? Neither do I. *(the party on the other end evidently hangs up. He jiggles the receiver-rest)* Hello...Hello! *(he hangs up and turns to Mary)* Now did I say anything that would insult a lady?
MARY: No—I thought you were awful sweet to her.
CAREY: That's my trouble. Just sweet. I was going to take a lady to the Opening. I forgot to go get her. And she forgot to be a lady.
MARY: But, Mr. Carey, people don't realize you're a genius.
CAREY: Do you know something? I once proposed to a woman for saying just that. *(sadly)* Then she turned around and sued me for fifty grand.
MARY: Sued you for being a genius?
CAREY: No. Sued me for fifty thousand dollars.
MARY: Anyway, you got a lot on the ball and don't let anybody kid you.
CAREY: You're the smartest girl I met tonight. When I ordered six glasses you brought 'em and didn't ask what for? Or did you? Well, now I'm going to ask you something else, and don't ask me what for? *(pauses)* Will you go with me to the Opening of my picture?

11

MARY: *(takes it big)* I've never been to an Opening, I mean, of course I'll go. But what will people think?
CAREY: Thinking is a lost art.
MARY: I haven't got any evening clothes, but I got the cutest dress. Just like the one Jean Summers wears. Gee! Will I go! And you won't be ashamed of me. I got plenty of ambition. I don't know it all, but I catch on. I'll go change. Where'll I meet you? Down at the corner?
CAREY: Out in front at my car.
   Mary puts his bill on table. She goes out. Carey rises, squints at bill, and moves toward door.

CUT TO EXTERIOR BROWN DERBY—NIGHT
Medium shot. Uniformed doorman is just closing somebody's car door. Car drives off. Carey comes from restaurant.
DOORMAN: Taxi, Mr. Carey?
CAREY: No. Where's my car?
DOORMAN: Don't you remember, Mr. Carey? You sent your car away with the old flower woman.
CAREY: *(remembering)* Oh. *(he looks off and sees:)*

EXTERIOR STREET—BROWN DERBY—NIGHT
Medium shot. A battered Ford is stalled about eight feet off the curb and other cars are trying to pass it and honking. A man is trying to crank it, sweating and swearing. He gets so mad he kicks the tire. Carey enters the scene.
CAREY: If she turns over, I'll buy her.
   The man gives him a look, then gives the car a mighty heave and she turns over.
CAREY: *(continued)* Ah! How much?
MAN: Well, would thirty-five dollars be too steep?
CAREY: Make it fifty and I'll take it. *(he peels off three bills and hands to man)*

CUT TO EXTERIOR STOCK SHOT GRAUMAN'S CHIN-ESE—OPENING—NIGHT
This shot is for atmospheric purposes and build-up for the

12

evening's progression. Actual scenes, stock shots, people at micro-phone, but no identifications.

CUT TO INTERIOR BROWN DERBY RESTAURANT—NIGHT
The locker room in Brown Derby. Mary is almost dressed to go out. Another waitress is there.
WAITRESS: You're not going to the opening dressed like that?
MARY: Why not? You got to be different to be a success in Hollywood. And I'm stepping out with the big shot that gave birth to this opera. Baby, won't I look swell—riding up in a Rolls-Royce!
WAITRESS: I will admit I never seen anybody look *bad* in a Rolls.
MARY: And you never will.
Nick comes in.
NICK: *(to Mary)* Why ain't you out there tending to business?
MARY: Nick, I just been invited to the opening.
NICK: All right, Miss Hollywood. If that's the way you feel. You're all washed up. Through.
MARY: *(sweeping grandly from the room; speaking as tough as nails)* In your Brown Derby!

CUT TO EXTERIOR BROWN DERBY—NIGHT
Carey and Mary. There is a dilapidated Ford at the curb. An open car that looks as though it had lost the World War. Carey bows and offers to hand Mary into the car. Carey wears his monocle here and in earlier shots.
MARY: *(rather suspicious)* What is this, a gag?
CAREY: No.
MARY: You taking me just for a laugh?
CAREY: No. Honest. I sent the old flower woman home and forgot all about it. You know? I saw this standing here and bought it. Fifty bucks. Come on, get in. You know the motto of Hollywood—it's all in fun.
MARY: All right. I'll hold it together while you drive.
They get in and the car starts off.
Sound—Motor starting

LAP DISSOLVE OUT

LAP DISSOLVE IN

EXTERIOR CHINESE THEATER—NIGHT
Full view of the crowd at the opening. General scene. Incidental voices of announcers against noises of crowd.
INCIDENTAL NOISES: Listen, folks, here comes Richard Dix and his beautiful wife.
Here is James K. McGuinness, Supervisor of "State's Attorney."
The celebrities are coming so thick and fast, it's hard to tell the thick from the fast.

CUT TO EXTERIOR CHINESE THEATER—NIGHT
Medium close shot—Carey and Mary in traffic, with two extraordinarily fine cars before them at curb before theater.
Close up of Mary and Carey.
MARY: Gee, but you're swell. You let people laugh at you, and all the time you're laughing at *them*.
He gives her a grateful look, revealing that she has analyzed his character perfectly.

CUT TO EXTERIOR CHINESE THEATER—NIGHT
Close shot—Looking toward curb with people approaching a microphone beside which stands a woman who has the appearance of an actress after age has caught up with her.
ANNOUNCER: Miss Kitty Knickerbocker will again take over the microphone and describe a few of the creations these beautiful, gorgeous stars are wearing to the opening of this epic,—colossal, terrific masterpiece. Miss Kitty...
MISS KITTY: Miss Georgia Van Raalte, the ingenue of this picture is wearing...
(Note: Miss Pemberton will oblige with description)

CUT TO EXTERIOR CHINESE THEATER—NIGHT
Medium shot. The Star, Alice Durant, is being helped out of her car by two attendants. There is much applause. Saxe gets out of car after her.

Sound—Applause
Alice gets out, bows, more applause. Her car pulls out. As she
comes closer, it is seen that she has much too many orchids. Saxe is
escorting her. A close shot shows him beaming. As they walk, they
hear a terrific peal of laughter. They both turn.
ALICE: That fool!
SAXE: I tell you, he's a genius.
The camera follows Saxe and Alice a short way and then pans back,
holding scene at curb, where Carey is handing Mary from the car.
There is much excitement and honking of horns.
Sound—Honking of horns and laughter
ATTENDANT: But, Mr. Carey. *(he is flustered)* You can't leave your car
there.
CAREY: *(walking away)* My good fellow, it's yours.
ATTENDANT: But I have a car.
CAREY: This one's paid for.

CUT TO EXTERIOR CHINESE THEATER—NIGHT
Saxe and Alice at microphone.
ALICE: *(very low, lazy voice)* Hello, everybody. Everybody, hello.
Charmed.
ANNOUNCER: And now, ladies and gentlemen, I wish to introduce the
man who produced this epic picture. Mr. Julius Saxe, owner of Olympic
Pictures.
SAXE: *(excited)* Hello, everybody. Hello, Mama. Oh, Mama, the picture
is going to be a big success. It is terrific. Sold out for a week in advance. I
am glad to tell you this, Mama. I hope this makes your rheumatism feel
better. Now everybody come see "Secret Love" and get an education. I
am the only producer that thinks the audience is older than fourteen. I
think the audience is nineteen at the very most. Goodnight, Mama. You
can go to bed now.
While Saxe is talking the camera pulls back and includes Carey and
Mary.
Saxe by now is in the seventh heaven. He notices Carey, who stands
dourly beside Mary. Saxe even smiles at Mary. Mary is holding
Carey's hand in a forthright, girlish fashion.

SAXE: *(continued) (to Carey)* Oh, there is Max Carey, my genius director. He vill say a few vurds. Maxie, say something over the microscope.

CAREY: My dear friends, I owe all my success to Beef, Iron and Wine. *(he gives a raucous raspberry)*
    He is about to continue when the microphone-man hastily intervenes.

ANNOUNCER: Excuse the static, folks.

CAREY: That wasn't static. *(Mary is laughing)* Now, I'll introduce that great heroine, Mademoiselle from Armentiers. *(turns to Mary)*

MARY: *(over mike)* Legionaires, I'm sorry I'm not really Mademoiselle from Armentiers that you sang so much about in the war. I'm just Mary Evans, and some day I hope you'll sing about my dramatic ability like you did about Mademoiselle's cooking. I thank you all. *(she turns and pauses. She looks off)*

CUT TO EXTERIOR CHINESE THEATER—NIGHT
A close shot of Kitty Knickerbocker eyeing Mary's plain outfit and shaking her head. She is describing the outfit of the star over a separate hook-up. (Miss Pemberton will again oblige) This description has been heard as a tonal background, faintly, during Scene 32.

CUT TO EXTERIOR CHINESE THEATER—NIGHT
MARY: *(continued) (speech as though continued over mike from Scene 34)* And I suppose, friends you want to know what I am wearing tonight. Well, it's a rather simple little ensemble, in very good taste. *(Details to be supplied by Mrs. Pemberton and ending with:)* And what's more, I earned the money to buy the material and then made it myself. So don't believe all the bad things you hear about Hollywood.

FADE OUT

FADE IN

EXTERIOR CAREY'S APARTMENT—DAY
On top of a hill.

LAP DISSOLVE

16

INTERIOR CAREY'S BEDROOM—DAY

Carey is asleep, partly dressed in trousers and dress shirt, with bare feet and a monocle in his eyes. We don't see the front of his shirt at this point.

As we fade in the telephone is ringing. It rings twice. Carey opens one eye and then reaches over and removes receiver, dropping it on the table. Then he groans and turns over.

CUT TO INTERIOR CORNER OF HALL—DAY

James, a valet and general houseman, is answering telephone.

JAMES: Yes, Mr. Saxe. He's still sleeping, Mr. Saxe. ... Oh, no, not intoxicated, merely exhausted, sir. ... I'll give him all your messages as soon as he wakes up. *(or)* Yes, Mr. Saxe. He's still sleeping. ... Oh, no, not unconscious... sleeping like a baby. But I'll give him *all* your messages as soon as he wakens.

He hangs up with a look of comic despair and starts out.

CUT TO INTERIOR CAREY'S BEDROOM—DAY

Carey is slowly getting out of bed in a half daze. He wets his lips sourly. James enters.

JAMES: Good morning, Mr. Carey. Mr. Saxe has called several times. He seemed in quite a temper.

CAREY: Good! Maybe he'll have apoplexy.

Carey goes into the bathroom and James, seeing the telephone receiver off, replaces it.

CUT TO INTERIOR CAREY'S APARTMENT—BATH-ROOM—DAY

Carey is preparing for a gargle. At the beginning of this shot, we see him before his bathroom medicine closet (over washbowl). The door of the closet is open and Carey is selecting a tremendously large bottle of Listerine. He does not bother to get glass, but takes a slug of Listerine and starts gargling as he shuts medicine closet door. He sets down the great bottle as the door closes and he glimpses self in mirror. He sees some handwriting on his shirt front and is puzzled, as it is (of course) in reverse in

17

mirror. Evidently thinking he has the jitters, he knocks over the huge bottle.
Sound—of dropping bottle and crash of glass
Then he spurts the Listerine against mirror and carefully picks way through broken glass. (Shot of scared feet on tiled floor, with shades of glass showing) James comes into scene. He is carrying a whiskey bottle.

CUT TO INTERIOR CAREY'S APARTMENT—MORNING
James and Carey at bathroom door, the latter is terrified.
CAREY: James, did I cut my feet—I'm afraid to look?
JAMES: *(looks down)* I don't see any cuts, sir.
CAREY: *(takes bottle and drinks)* James—*(gestures to shirt-front)*—will you read this fan letter?
Note: Make conform to Miss Bennett
JAMES: *(reading while Carey is drinking)* "Mary Evans. Five feet, three inches, weight 102 pounds, complexion blonde, sings and swims, rides horseback. Telephone: Gladstone 5309."
CAREY: *(takes pencil from James' breast pocket. Holds bottle up to light, squints, then carefully marks it at liquor level, and gives James a knowing look)* I wonder who...
JAMES: It must have been the young lady.
CAREY: *(hands bottle and pencil back to James)* Did I bring somebody home last night?
JAMES: No, sir. Somebody brought you home this morning. *(James nods his head, off)* She's asleep in the library.
James goes out. Carey looks mystified. He glances at his bed and then at the door. He picks up a dressing gown.

CUT TO INTERIOR CAREY'S APARTMENT—MORNING
The alcove where Carey's liquor cabinet is located. James is about to put the bottle in closet. He looks around knowingly, then examines mark on label, takes a healthful swig, remarks the bottle and puts it away. The telephone rings off scene. James goes to answer.

CUT TO INTERIOR CAREY'S APARTMENT—MORNING

The Library. Mary is asleep, curled up in a huge chair. A robe of coyote skins, really a rug, is draped over her. Carey is leaning above her. He watches her for a few moments. She rouses, seems at sea.

MARY: *(gives a little start)* Oh...

CAREY: What's new? Did you have a nice sleep?

MARY: I've only been asleep a little while. I was out on your verandah looking at the city lights. Gee, it's swell up here on the mountain. So clean and quiet.

CAREY: Just what happened last night?

MARY: Oh, nothing. You passed out in the middle of the picture.

CAREY: Was it that bad?

MARY: It was well directed, but that dame! And was she leg-conscious!
    James enters, apologetically.

JAMES: Excuse me, sir. It's Mr. Saxe again. He asks what you're doing?

CAREY: Well, James, you tell him we're all having a wonderful time and we wish he were here and I'll write later.

JAMES: *(calmly)* Thank you, sir. *(he withdraws)*

CAREY: *(turns to Mary)* Didn't I insult somebody last night? I've a vague memory of...

MARY: Nobody but Muto. You tripped him when he was walking down the aisle. And, boy, was I worried you'd lose your monocle!

CAREY: *(laughs—then, frankly)* May I ask you something very personal?

MARY: Why not?

CAREY: Just *where* and *how* did I meet you?

MARY: At the Brown Derby. I bought you from another waitress.

CAREY: Bought me? *(remembering)* Oh, yes... you work there.

MARY: No. I did, but I gave up my job for you, palsy-walsy.

CAREY: *(pours drink from decanter on low table. Sits on arm of chair. There is a French telephone on the table)* Well...

MARY: I suppose you want to know how I got up here? You were plastered. I brought you home in a cab. The driver and I carried you up this mountain. All *you* did was yodel. A big help!

CAREY: And you were so charmed by my yodeling you couldn't leave me.

MARY: Well, I'm looking for a break in pictures. I thought you might give me a chance.

CAREY: What do you know about that?

MARY: Well, I'm no wise guy, but I believe in myself. All I need is a break. *(notices him as he keeps pouring drinks)* Anyway, do you have to drink all the time? Why don't you stop the heavy swilling?

CAREY: What? And be bored *all* the time? Ever work in pictures?

MARY: Not yet. But I keep hanging around Central Casting. Say, will you write them a letter for me?

CAREY: I'll do better than that. You're a great kid. I yodeled, did I? I didn't do anything else ... I mean ...

MARY: I know what you mean. No. And it was a novelty.

CAREY: *(rather sadly)* I guess I'm slipping. Well, what's new? I'll tell you. You come to the studio tomorrow morning and come on my set.

MARY: Gee, that's great!

CAREY: Now, I'm sending you home in my car. *(very confidentially)* I'm giving you my telephone number, and don't spill it. *(he thinks a while)* Know something? I forgot it. Anyway, look it up in the book. It's listed under the name of my Chinese cook, Hip Song Lung. You think I'm screwy, don't you?

   Sound—Telephone rings.

MARY: No, I know you're screwy. *(she kisses him on the cheek)*
   Then she goes into hall and yodels. Carey yodels back.
   Sound—The telephone rings.

FADE OUT

FADE IN

EXTERIOR STREET—DAY
James is at wheel of Carey's Rolls-Royce. Mary is seated grandly. She looks in purse and finds only a quarter. She speaks to James through the tube.

MARY: *(very ritzy)* James, will you stop at the Brown Derby and go in and ask for Mary Evan's paycheck? *(James nods) (she hangs up and continues to wallow in grandeur—she finds mirror and compact in side fixture—she fondles compact—she takes the powder puff, dabs her cheek, looks in mirror; into mirror)* Mary, you look like dog meat this morning.

Mary finds an elaborate and huge cigarette case. She opens it to discover an assortment of brands. She takes a cigarette and then uses the car lighter. The car halts before the Brown Derby. A uniformed "Buttons" comes forward but James gets out and goes into restaurant. Buttons gets an eyeful of Mary, looks amazed and dashes into restaurant.

CUT TO INTERIOR BROWN DERBY—DAY
Shooting towards the street as James enters and goes to Manager's Office. Buttons comes to the cash counter and speaks to the cigarette girl. Nick is standing there. Nick and the girl look out in amazement, where they see the Rolls-Royce.
BUTTONS: Get a load of that, will you?
They all register amazement and incredulity.
NICK: *(slapping his chest)* You see—when they work for me, they get someplace...
James approaches him...

CUT TO EXTERIOR BROWN DERBY—DAY
Muto sees Mary in the Rolls. He's holding some papers in his hands. He has other copies in his pocket.
MUTO: Well, well, sister. You've put in a good night's work.
MARY: Are you selling papers, my good man!
MUTO: No, Lady! I write 'em...and you can consider yourself a success. You've finally hit my column.
He hands her a copy. She takes it. Muto still watching her.

CUT TO
*Insert closeup of Muto's paper, THE HOLLYWOOD TATTLER
Muto's column:*

> *"Reeling Around Hollywood"*
> *(Cut of Muto in body-type)*
> "Producer Saxe's latest atrocity 'Secret Love' wobbled all over

the screen last night. In fairness to Director Carey, he didn't wander as much as usual. But he is slipping.

By the way, who was the little blonde that acted as his main crutch at the opening? No doubt she is familiar to diners at the Brown Derby. Heigho!"

EXTERIOR STREET—AT CAR—DAY

Mary folds the paper and without a word daintily drops it in the gutter.

James comes from restaurant with some money which he hands to Mary.

JAMES: He said you only had six-fifty coming, Miss.

MARY: *(takes money)* To my town house, James.

EXTERIOR STREET—DAY

Longer shot—James bows and takes his place at the wheel and they drive off.

FADE OUT

FADE IN

EXTERIOR SAXE STUDIO—DAY

LAP DISSOLVE

EXTERIOR LOT—DAY

With certain amount of activity.

LAP DISSOLVE

EXTERIOR LOT—DAY

Medium close shot—of Mary walking along, a pink studio pass in her hand. She is overawed by this place she has dreamed about. She looks off and sees:

EXTERIOR LOT—DAY

Pan shots of Administration Building, Projection Building, Film Vaults, Camera Building, Wardrobe, etc. People hurrying in and out. Mary's eager eyes take in everything—a big truck passes her, loaded with extras in costume. The next moment she hears a voice yell:

VOICE: Hot points!

Mary moves aside to let a cameraman pass. He carries his tripod over his shoulder. Sound trucks pass, a beautiful star passes, accompanied by her maid, with make-up box. Two still cameramen are shooting publicity pictures of some bathing girls.

Mary walks on and comes to entrance of stage. A bell rings, but the door is open, and timidly she enters and looks about, as though she were in a Cathedral. The stage is enormous and at the extreme end, Carey is rehearsing his company. Mary starts toward them. The attendant closes the door behind Mary. More bells ring.

CUT TO INTERIOR SOUND STAGE—DAY

Medium shot—Carey is watching as a scene is being shot. The cameras are turning. The actors are speaking their lines.

CLARICE: But I saw you kiss her.

CLARK: I was only sorry for her. I'd do as much for any girl.

CAREY: Cut. *(boy runs out with scene numbers)* How was it for sound?

VOICE: O.K. for sound.

ELECTRICIAN: Kill 'em.

Lights go out.

CAREY: That's all for today.

INTERIOR SOUND STAGE—DAY

Medium shot—Saxe jumps up as he hears Carey speak. Mary arrives at the edge of the group. Saxe goes to Carey.

INTERIOR SOUND STAGE—DAY

Closer Shot

SAXE: Why you say that's all for today?

23

CAREY: *(very nasty)* Because I said three hundred extras on the set at nine o'clock and they're not here.

SAXE: *(with growing indignation)* Yes, and you said three hundred extras on the set yesterday morning and *you* weren't here! What kind of monkeyshines is this—You're driving me crazy! I should pay three hundred extras seven dollars and a half a day while yo.ı sleep off a drunk! D'you know how much is three hundred times seven and a half?

CAREY: No, and neither do you. I'm a director, not a bookkeeper. And if you want me to finish this masterpiece, give me what I ask for and *stay off the set!*

SAXE: Three hundred extras is too many . . . a thousand times too many! I give you twenty-five.

CAREY: And you expect me to shoot an Embassy Ball with twenty-five people! Maybe you want me to play it in a telephone booth.

SAXE: All right. This once I give in to you. You can *have* a hundred and fifty extras. *(he stamps off)*

CAREY: *(calling after him)* Make 'em all twins! *(then he motions to Assistant)* My tea.

> *Prop boy dashes up with a cup of whiskey. Carey looks at him and grunts inquiringly. Prop boy nods. Carey drinks. At this moment, Mary steps up beside Carey and speaks.*

MARY: *(brightly)* Hello, Mr. Carey.

CAREY: *(looks at her blankly a minute)* What's your name again?

MARY: *(a bit crestfallen)* Mary Evans. *(and she yodels softly)*

CAREY: Oh . . . it's you! That's right! Jimmie!

> *Assistant hurries in.*

JIMMIE: Yes, sir.

CAREY:This's Miss Evans—for that bit part on the stairs. Take her to the wardrobe and pick out a good-looking evening dress for her. Have her on the set, made up, at eight this evening.

JIMMIE: Yes, sir. *(to Mary)* Come on.

MARY: Thank you, Mr. Carey.

JIMMIE: Come on! Snap into it!

> *He starts off. Mary runs a couple of steps to catch up with him. Carey takes another drink.*

FADE OUT

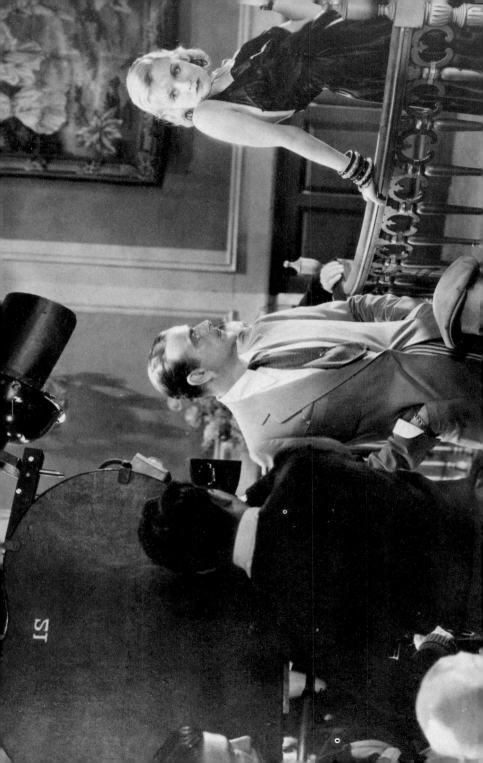

FADE IN

INTERIOR STAIRWAY SET—NIGHT
Mary, Carey, Assistant and others ready to start scene. Carey turns to Electrician.
CAREY: Let's have that baby spot. We'll rehearse this once more before we take it. You know what you have to do, Miss Evans.
MARY: Yes, sir, I think so.
CAREY: D'you know your line?
MARY: *(without any attempt at inflection)* Hello, Buzzy, you haven't proposed to me yet tonight.
CAREY: That's right. Take your position half-way up the stairs.
Mary goes halfway up the stairs and takes her position. The actor, Clark, comes and stands at the foot of the stairs.
CAREY: *(continued) (calls)* All right, Miss Evans, come on.
Mary walks down the stairs, her knees shaking. She hangs onto the rail to help herself, then lets go. At the bottom, Clark steps forward to meet her. Mary manages to articulate the line.
MARY: *(darkly)* Hello Buzzy. You haven't proposed to me yet tonight.
Then she is supposed to see someone off the scene and her face must register fright. She does her best with it.
CLARK: What is it Rosemary? Are you ill? *(then they stop and look at Carey. Pause)*
CAREY: Yes. Suppose we try it once more. Come down the stairs lightly, gracefully... Don't hang onto the rail... you're sober... and speak your line with more animation. Put a little zip into it ... now remember you're a good looking wench and you're going to make this poor sap down here propose to you. Now let's try it. *(Mary goes back up and waits for Carey to speak)* All right. Come on. *(Mary takes about three steps when he stops her)* Go back. Now don't walk on your heels, *please,* and don't clench your fists. This isn't a fight, it's a love scene. Come on... be gay... smile...
Mary comes down the stairs, obviously on her toes, with a funny springy movement. At the bottom Clark meets her.
MARY: *(with a frightened grin)* Hello Buzzy. You haven't proposed to me yet tonight. (she giggles out consciously, then looks up, and her face changes to what she thinks is horror)*

25

CLARK:What is it Rosemary? Are you ill?
CAREY: All right. Wrap 'em up. We'll take it in the morning. *(to Assistant)* You better line up another gal for me.
ASSISTANT: Yes, sir.
   Mary hears and touches Carey's arm. He turns and sees her.
MARY: I wasn't very good, was I?
CAREY: Oh, you were all right. Now you mustn't be discouraged. You keep in touch with me. I may have something else for you someday.
MARY: *(lips trembling a bit)* I think I could do it better tomorrow.
CAREY: *(reaching in his pocket)* That reminds me—you said you left your job. Here's some money. You're going to get along fine.
MARY: *(with her pride to the rescue)* Thanks, but I have plenty of money. Good night.
CAREY: *(pleasantly)* Good night. Let me know what's new.
   Mary hurries away.
ASSISTANT: How many extras for tomorrow, Mr. Carey?
CAREY: Three hundred.
ASSISTANT: Yes, sir.

CUT TO INTERIOR STUDIO—NIGHT
Traveling close shot—Mary stumbles along, blinded by tears, passing a wall and reaches the revolving gate. Place camera for a straight-on shot and show her come through the gate, pause and try to go back—sees the gate only works one way. Stands looking back a moment, then, still weeping, hurries off.

LAP DISSOLVE

EXTERIOR MARY'S APARTMENT BUILDING—NIGHT
Mary, with dragging feet, comes to front door and goes inside.

CUT TO INTERIOR HALLWAY—NIGHT
Mary slowly ascends the stairs. Halfway up, she gets an idea. She turns and starts gaily down the stairs. As she does so, we see the landlady come from a door at the rear, reaching the bottom of the stairs just as Mary does.

LANDLADY: *(who has once been in pictures herself)* Hello, Mary. How did you get along at the Studio today?
MARY: *(enthusiastically)* Oh, swell, Mrs. Bangs. I did a bit. I wouldn't be surprised if I got a contract.
LANDLADY: Now, don't be too quick signing up, dearie. You might do better free lancing. *(she goes into room at bottom of stairs)*
Mary runs up the stairs and starts doggedly rehearsing her scene. As she comes down the stairs and says—
MARY: Don't walk on your heels...don't clench your fists...be gay...smile...let go the rail...smile... *(and does she smile. At the foot of the stairs she says)* Hello, Buzzy. You haven't proposed to me yet tonight.
A clock in a tower begins to boom out eleven o'clock, at beginning of scene.

LAP DISSOLVE

CLOSE SHOT—FACE OF CLOCK—NIGHT
The hands move from 11 to 12 and strike. Then to one, and strike.

LAP DISSOLVE

INTERIOR HALLWAY—NIGHT
Mary coming down the stairs, lightly and gracefully. At the foot of the stairs she says her line perfectly—provocatively.
MARY: Hello, Buzzy. You haven't proposed to me yet tonight.
Then she sees the imaginary person and a look of fear and horror come over her face—

CUT TO INTERIOR FRONT DOOR—NIGHT
Half open, and in it stands the actor to whom she gave the quarter. He applauds with evident sincerity.

CUT TO INTERIOR HALLWAY—NIGHT
Mary, smiling, pleased with herself.
MARY: *(continued)* Will that knock him dead tomorrow morning? or

27

Wait till he asks me what's new tomorrow! *(she nods her head as if to say, "I'll show him," and starts up the stairs)*

FADE OUT

FADE IN

INTERIOR PROJECTION ROOM NO. 3
The scene fades in during the projection of rushes. It is a Chinese war drama. As the scene fades in, some wicked-looking Chinamen are shown shooting machine guns towards audience.
Sound—Machine gun fire
The scene in the foreground is dim. We see silhouettes only of heads.
A door opens. We hear Saxe's voice. He is angry.
SAXE: Who's there? Lights. *(the lights go up)*
We see Mary, who has wandered in.
SAXE: *(continued)* *(thunders at Mary)* What you coming in for? Who are you? Huh? Get out!
MARY: I'm sorry. *(she leaves)*

INTERIOR PROJECTION BOOTH
Mary shown in projection machine booth, peeking through at her picture as it is being run.

CUT TO INTERIOR PROJECTION ROOM
The lights go off and the rushes continue. This time the rushes are the scenes Carey shot with Clarice and Clark followed by the bit with Mary and Clark.
On the screen Mary comes downstairs, Clark meets her and it is all done exactly as we saw Mary rehearse it on her stairs.
Dialogue on screen:
MARY: Hello, Buzzie. You haven't proposed to me yet tonight.
CLARK: What's the matter, Rosemary? Are you ill?
A man with slate comes before camera and is shown on screen.
SAXE: *(excitedly)* Terrific! Who's that gorgeous creature?
The lights go up.

CAREY: That's the little girl you just threw out.

SAXE: Sign her up immediately *(turns to his secretary)* Make a note of that, Miss Spiegel.

MISS SPIEGEL: *(she has a bottle and a spoon—he pours a spoonful of medicine and gives it to Saxe)* Yes, sir.

SAXE: Maybe she's a big discovery. *(to Miss Spiegel)* Tell them to run it over again so I can see the girl.

Miss Spiegel goes to telephone on table and rings.

CUT TO INTERIOR PROJECTION MACHINE BOOTH

Sound—The telephone rings. The operator lifts the receiver.

OPERATOR: Okay. *(he looks wisely at Mary and hangs up)* He wants to look at your stuff again. It's a good sign.

Close shot of Mary. Her face is a study of happiness.

MARY: *(incredulously and amazed)* Gee. That's me talking! *(her voice from screen carries over her remark)*

CUT TO INTERIOR PROJECTION ROOM

Saxe and Carey are sitting together. Cecil is taking dictation.

SAXE: *(finishing a cable)* Send this cable to our London office, too. What's a big word for collosal?

MISS SPIEGEL: Tremendous.

SAXE: No. That belongs to the Burner Brothers Studio. Take it. Have just seen rushes of Chinese picture and it is positively stupendous.

MISS SIEGEL: Stupendous.

SAXE: I like stupendous better'n tremendous, don't you, Carey?

CAREY: One's as bad as the other. They use them both to describe flops.

SAXE: Make it "terrific." It sounds successful. Terrific box-office. Terrific crowds. Terrific talent. That's the word. Terrific. To our New York office, copies Mr. Huliban, Mr. Grossmiller, Mr. (...)well, to everybody. Our new Picture, "Clouds over China" is terrific. This should bring standing lines back to our theaters. It is terrific. *(Carey starts out of door—Saxe to Carey)* Just a minute. Where's that girl I just threw out of here? *(to Miss Spiegel)* Make it a day letter.

CAREY: I don't know.

SAXE: Well, find her and bring her back.

29

CUT TO PROJECTION BOOTH

OPERATOR: He means you.

MARY: *(excited—hollers through aperture)* I'm here, Mr. Saxe. *(then she dashes out of booth)*

CUT TO PROJECTION ROOM

Saxe looks up at aperture as if he had heard something—he's not quite sure what. The next instant Mary dashes in.

MARY: Here I am, Mr. Saxe.

SAXE: Hm. Sit down. What's your name?

MARY: Mary Evans.

SAXE: Mary Evans. Well, we can change it.

CAREY: *(with irony)* But Mary is a grand old name, Saxie. Great box office.

SAXE: All right. We keep it. I give you seventy-five dollars a week for the first three months, a hundred for the next six months. One hundred and fifty for the next year, five hundred for the following year and a thousand a week after that until seven years. You're making a million dollars.

MARY: *(gasps)* A million dollars.

SAXE: And if you make good, I'll be the first to tear up your contract and give you raises. Here's a dollar in hand on a thirty-day option . . . that makes it legal. *(turns to Miss Spiegel)* Miss Spiegel, ring for all my heads of departments . . . and get Mama on the phone. I must tell her I discovered a new star . . .

CAREY: *Who* discovered a new star?

SAXE: Maximillian Carey discovered a new star . . . *(Saxe goes through his pockets for a piece of paper and pencil)*

CAREY: You're welcome.

SAXE: *(turns to Mary)* Your name . . . Mary Evans. *(writes it down)*
    While he is figuring on her name we hear Miss Spiegel's voice come over the scene.

MISS SPIEGEL'S VOICE: Mr. Saxe wants all department heads in Projection Room Three right away. And get Mama Saxe on the long distance . . . Medea Baths, Mt. Clemens, Michigan.

SAXE: It's all right. It comes out lucky. What day were you born?

MARY: August 26, 1912.

SAXE: *(calls)* Miss Spiegel.

MISS SPIEGEL'S VOICE: Yes, Mr. Saxe.

SAXE: *(takes his flower from buttonhole, smells it and returns it—Miss Spiegel enters)* Her horoscope. She was born in August. Miss Spiegel knows all about horoscopes.

MISS SPIEGEL: Mr. Saxe, it's a terrific sign. The stars are all in tune. *The heads, meanwhile, have trooped in and are standings.*

SAXE: *(takes his flower out and smells it)* Gentlemen, the stars have decreed this young lady shall be a star of the highest magnitude.

CHORUS: Congratulations, Mr. Saxe.

SAXE: *(to Miss Spiegel)* Did you get Mama on the phone yet?

MISS SPIEGEL: *(goes to telephone; over phone)* Did you get Mama Saxe on the phone yet?

TWO MEN: How is your mother, Mr. Saxe?

SAXE: Thank you, gentlemen. Mama's rheumatism is better, but she should not travel before Venus crosses Mars. *(to Mary)* Mama's got rheumatism in Mt. Clemens. *(to the heads)* Now, gentlemen, I tell you what we should do. We start a national publicity campaign about Miss Evans... We make her a famous siren—a girl no man can resist... we give her a few lovers—not too many... just enough to make all the other women wonder how she does it... you, Donald, you think up a scandal we can publish about her... a nice respectable scandal that everybody'll like... if any rich man commits suicide in the next few weeks, publish a rumor she refused to marry him... Miss Spiegel, take a note. Get her a library. She reads only the Old Masters, Rex Beach, Rupert Hughes, Longfellow and Shakespeare, and some good Greek, Eugene O'Neill.

MISS SPIEGEL: Your mother, Mr. Saxe—on Number Seven.

SAXE: *(turning to a writer)* And Grover, I want you should write a story for Miss Evans... about a woman of flame. We got the best dialogue writer in New York coming next week. He will write the words. You don't have to do nothing but write the story, the business what they do and where they do it. This dialoguer will write everything they say. Can you do that, Grover?

GROVER: Write a story without any dialogue?

SAXE: That's right. No dialogue. *(he takes down receiver—is all excitement)* Mama. Is that you? Yes. Julius. I'm so lonesome. Great news, Mama. I'm creating a new star. She will be a siren, Mama.

31

(shouts) No, not a police siren, Mama, a young Dietrich. Another Duse, Garbo, all rolled up. Don't worry about the money. Sure it costs money for long distance. Don't worry, Mama. It's a modern age. I have all my heads here. They send their love, Mama. *(he looks at them and they all nod as he nods, in perfect time)* Good bye, Mama dear ... it's worth it. I love you. *(he hangs up)* A man's best friend is his Mama. *(to Treasurer)* Lease a house. Secluded and colossal. Call up the bank and get a house that's been foreclosed.

   Carey rises to leave.
MARY: Oh, Mr. Carey! I'm in pictures! *(throws arms about his neck)*
CAREY: Well, don't blame me.
SAXE: Don't go way, Carey. I want to have a talk with you. Goodbye, Mary.
MARY: Goodbye, Mr. Saxe. Goodbye, Mr. Carey.
CAREY: Goodbye, Mary. Watch your options, now. *(Mary goes out surrounded by heads of departments, all talking to her—Carey turns to Saxe)* Well, what's new?
SAXE: Carey, I like you. You're a fine director.
CAREY: All right. What have I done now?
SAXE: That's it. I'll tell you. You're slipping, Carey. All the time with a bottle ... all the time shiker ... no longer you care are the scenes good ... no longer you care is film being wasted ... all the time retakes ... all the time over schedule.
CAREY: *(with mock seriousness)* Well, now let's think a minute, Saxie ... Who can we get to take my place ...
SAXE: *(immediately conciliatory)* Now, I'm just telling you this for your own good, Carey. You're even losing your memory with this drinking business. You're getting mashugah. It's no good. You gotta stop. Five years ago you were ten years ahead of the business and now you're not quite even with it—and what's the answer? Whiskey!
CAREY: You're right, Saxie. What the picture business needs is light wines and beer. *(he gets up and reaches for a cigarette)*

FADE OUT

FADE IN

EXTERIOR POLO FIELD—DAY
Long shot—Picture troupe is on location in Santa Barbara. Some of the polo players on their ponies are practicing on the field. The Sound Truck and Cameras are in position. Carey is yelling instructions through a megaphone.

CUT TO EXTERIOR POLO FIELD—DAY
Medium shot—Mary and the other members of the company, in make-up, are eating their box lunches.
MARY: How is Three-Bottle Carey today?
1ST ACTOR: In his usual form.
ANOTHER ACTOR: This is the worst box lunch I've met up with yet.
1ST ACTOR: If you weren't here, you wouldn't be eating at all. Who wants an apple?
MARY: I do. *(Actor tosses it to her. She catches it expertly with one hand—does the imitation of Dietrich in "Morocco"—sings)* Vot am I bid for my apple? The fruit that made Adam so wise...

CUT TO EXTERIOR POLO FIELD—DAY
Medium shot—Clark, the leading man, in polo clothes and make-up, and a good-looking young chap also in polo clothes, but without make-up, are standing, watching Mary. Her voice in the rest of the song comes over this shot.
MARY'S VOICE: *(off scene—sings)*
BORDEN: *(admiringly)* Say, she's clever!
CLARK: *(a bit bored)* Oh, she's got something.
At this moment Carey enters scene.
CAREY: All right, Mr. Borden. Your team is all ready. Will you tell Mr. Clark what to do?
Borden turns and motions off scene to someone to bring their ponies. Then he turns to Clark.
BORDEN: D'you mind, Mr. Clark, if I show you how I hold the mallet? *(he demonstrates with his own mallet)* And wrap the thong about your thumb like this.

33

CLARK: Thanks, but I always hold it this way. *(has thong wrapped about wrist)*
BORDEN: I know, but if ycur mallet gets fouled with another mallet or your pony's legs, you're pulled off.
CAREY: That's right, Clark! You couldn't learn a thing from Mr. Borden. He's only the best polo player in the country.
CLARK: Well, I've played polo before myself.
> *Two ponies are led into scene. Borden mounts one, Clark the other.*

CUT TO EXTERIOR POLO FIELD—DAY
Medium close shot— Mary is seated before a make-up table, fixing her make-up. She looks up and sees Borden and Clark riding down the field.
MARY: There's that one that rides so well—Who is he?
MAID: Mr. Carey said that was Lonny Borden.
1ST ACTOR: Yes, that's Borden. He's a nine-goal man.
MARY: *(with renewed interest)* Oh, I *like* him! He makes my heart go potata—potata.

CUT TO EXTERIOR POLO FIELD—DAY
Long shot—Two teams go into action—some nice riding from Lonny Borden, and then suddenly a mix-up around Clark.

EXTERIOR POLO FIELD—DAY
Medium shot—Clark is pulled off his horse. Borden comes riding up and quickly dismounts. Carey comes running in.
BORDEN: I'm sorry—Are you all right?
CLARK: *(frostily)* Quite, thank you. *(He gets up, a bit dazed)*
CAREY: Sure you're not hurt, Roger?
CLARK: *(with dignity)* I'm quite all right.
BORDEN: *(sympathetically)* I'm afraid you held the mallet wrong—that's what I told you.
CLARK: Actors and children, Mr. Borden—You got to let 'em see for themselves.
BORDEN: Would you let my doctor look you over?
CLARK: No, thanks. I'll have my personal physician fly up from Hollywood. *(limps off toward his pony)*

BORDEN: But my doctor's an orthopedic specialist.

CAREY: His doctor is a brain specialist.

Mary enters scene—Borden is about to mount his pony.

MARY: *(to Carey)* Is he hurt?

CAREY: I don't think so. Oh, Miss Evans, this is Mr. Borden—Miss Evans is our leading lady.

BORDEN: You don't have to tell me, Carey. I'm an Evans' fan.

MARY: And I'm a Borden fan. Seeing you ride does something to me.

BORDEN: Seeing you on the screen does something to me.

CAREY: *(calling)* All right, Mr. Borden. Roger thinks he can finish the scene.

BORDEN: All right. *(he turns back to Mary)*

MARY: *(holding out her hand)* Goodbye, Mr. Borden.

BORDEN: *(taking her hand)* Don't say goodbye . . . May I come back?

MARY: Sure.

Borden smiles (and I mean smiles), mounts his pony and rides off.

EXTERIOR POLO FIELD—DAY

Longer shot—Borden rides into the center of the field and everybody takes his position. Ad lib talk.

EXTERIOR POLO FIELD—DAY

Medium close shot—Mary stands beside Carey, watching.

MARY: Is Lonny Borden married?

CAREY: No. He's strictly a breach of promise guy.

MARY: Think he'd go for me?

CAREY: Never heard of him refusing anybody.

MARY: What a man! *(pause) Look* at him *ride!*

CUT TO EXTERIOR POLO FIELD—DAY

Medium long shot—showing a spectacular ride with Lonny making a goal.

FADE OUT

FADE IN

INTERIOR MARY'S SUITE—SANTA BARBARA HOTEL—NIGHT
Mary and maid.
Sound—The telephone rings.
Servant answers telephone.
MAID: Who's calling? *(turns to Mary)* It's Mr. Borden. *(into phone)* She's busy now, could she call you back? *(listens—then to Mary)* Mr. Borden wants to know if you'll come to his bungalow for a cocktail— Mr. Carey is there?
MARY: Tell him "yes."

CUT TO INTERIOR BORDEN'S BUNGALOW—NIGHT
Borden and Carey. Carey is slopped up.
BORDEN: What sort of person is this Miss Evans?
CAREY: Don't ask me. If I start talking about her, I'm liable to shout myself sober.
BORDEN: But, is she involved anywhere... Part of anybody's pattern?
CAREY: Mary's the kind of girl the next morning you could tell your mother what happened the night before.
BORDEN: What's your intererst in her?
CASEY: My interest in Mary? You wouldn't understand it. *(he passes out on couch)*
Mary enters. Borden rises.
BORDEN: Oh, hello!
Mary goes over to Carey. One of his legs is hanging off couch. She lifts his foot and straightens him generally on the couch.
CAREY: *(mumbling—referring to his leg)* I been... wanting... to do that... for a ong time...
BORDEN: *(offering Mary a chair. She sits down)* Want a highball or a cocktail, Mary?
MARY: May I have a glass of ginger ale?
BORDEN: *(sitting beside her)* Don't you drink?
MARY: Sure I do. But not just to be drinking.
BORDEN: You needn't be afraid of the liquor.
MARY: I'm not afraid of anything.

BORDEN: Then we'll have dinner served here.

MARY: Let's go where there's a crowd.

BORDEN: *(studies her)* Then you *are* afraid?

MARY: No. I'd just like to dance—with you.

BORDEN: All right. *(looks at Carey)* What'll I do with our horizontal friend?

MARY: Let him sleep. But take all his matches away. Last winter he set fire to Napoleon's bed in Mr. Saxe's Beverly Hills home.

> *They go out. After a moment the telephone rings insistently. Carey rouses and answers.*

CAREY: *(half-conscious)* Who d'you want... huh? Long distance... Who?... Mr. Carey?... Mr. Carey?... Oh, yes, this is Mr. Carey... Oh, it's you, Saxie. Good old Saxie... what's new?

CUT TO TELEPHONE—HOLLYWOOD
Saxe is talking into phone.

SAXE: There's nothin' new. Yesterday you were five days behind schedule. Today you're seven days behind. There's nothin' new about that... huh?... Sure I saw the rushes... and I want to ask you, Carey,— why is it you go to film a polo game and in the background you show cows and sheep eatin' grass? The script don't say nothing about wild animals...

INTERIOR BORDEN'S BUNGALOW—NIGHT
Carey at telephone.

CAREY: What script? I never read any script... Listen, Saxie, why d'you bother me when I'm working so hard...

CUT TO TELEPHONE—HOLLYWOOD—NIGHT
Saxe at telephone.

SAXE: That's right, Carey, you are working too hard—you ought to get a long rest. Suppose I send up another director to finish the picture... what d'you say?

CUT TO INTERIOR BORDEN'S BUNGALOW—NIGHT
Carey at telephone.

CAREY: I say nerts! *(he hangs up the receiver—looks around, sees a bottle and starts for it)*

FADE OUT

FADE IN

INTERIOR SANTA BARBARA HOTEL SUPPER ROOM—NIGHT

Borden and Mary are at the table. The place is far from full. The few persons present are of a stilted, social order, the majority of them elderly. A rather dignified string orchestra is sawing out aged dance tunes. The dance floor is all but deserted. A fogey couple are walking through the waltz. At a table some distance from Mary and Borden, and sitting at Borden's back, is an old goof in stiff evening array. He is alone.

BORDEN: D'you want to dance?

MARY: *(with a nice smile)* No.

BORDEN: You want to eat some more?

MARY: *(different inflection)* No.

BORDEN: Want to go for a walk in the moonlight?

MARY: *(looking at him with a little grin)* No.

BORDEN: Now you ask one.

CUT TO INTERIOR SANTA BARBARA HOTEL SUPPER ROOM—NIGHT

Elderly Guest as he flips another cracker, this time catching it in his mouth. His mouth shuts like a trap and he beams, just as Borden, following Mary's gaze, looks around. Both laugh.

MARY: Who is that goof juggling his dinner?

BORDEN: That's John Appelby, Jr.

MARY: Junior! How old is his father?

BORDEN: Nobody cares. He's got a hundred million dollars. Now, don't you wish we'd eaten in my bungalow?

MARY: Yes.

BORDEN: Then why didn't you?

38

MARY: I don't know. Why do people do lots of things? Why do people worth a hundred million snap at oyster crackers?
BORDEN: *(irrelevantly)* You know, I could like you an awful lot.
MARY: Anything stopping you?
BORDEN: Let's get out of here. *(they rise and move away from table)*

LAP DISSOLVE

EXTERIOR BEACH—NIGHT
Mary and Borden walking along. They come to a romantic spot.
BORDEN: Let's stop here.
MARY: It's a beautiful night!
BORDEN: *(his voice is colored with feeling)* Let's stop, Mary.
MARY: *(stops long enough to say—)* Lonny, I don't want to be just another girl and another night to you. *(then she walks on—he follows beside her)*
BORDEN: Mary, does every fool you meet go off his head about you like I have?
MARY: *(smiling teasingly)* Lonny! Would you call him a fool if he did?
BORDEN: *(grabbing her fiercely)* Yes, if he let you laugh at him!
MARY: *(swept by his emotion)* I'm ... not laughing, Lonny.
BORDEN: Mary! Couldn't you like me a little?
MARY: *(trying to get back to the kidding footing)* Maybe I could like you a lot ... if you wouldn't mind letting me breathe while I consider it ... *(he releases her a little—she smiles)* Thanks. *(moves her body from side to side)* Not a bone broken either ...
BORDEN: Will you be serious or have I got to drown myself?
MARY: That's an idea. Come one. *(she grabs his hand and starts to run toward the water's edge)*

CUT TO EXTERIOR ROW OF CABANAS
Mary and Borden run into scene.
MARY: This is mine. Carey's is next door. You'll find a bathing suit in it. *(she moves to go into her cabana, but he still holds her hand—tries to draw her up to him, but she stops him)* We're going *swimming!* *(she breaks away and goes inside cabana. Borden runs to the one next door.)*

CUT TO INTERIOR CABANA
Mary turns on a table flashlight and finds bathing suit. She hurriedly removes her clothes.

LAP DISSOLVE

EXTERIOR WATER'S EDGE—NIGHT
Mary and Borden are running toward the water hand in hand. As they hit the water Mary stops and chatters.
MARY: Ugh! It's cold.
BORDEN: *(grabbing her hand)* Come on! Get wet!
They wade out and dive into the surf. Stay with them a few moments and then—

LAP DISSOLVE OUT

LAP DISSOLVE IN

EXTERIOR RAFT—MOONLIGHT
Mary and Borden swim to the raft. As he climbs aboard and helps her on, he says:
BORDEN: Here we are. We got the whole ocean to ourselves.
They sit, feet in water. His arm goes about her. Suddenly he kisses her throat back of one ear.
MARY: Lonny. One of us has got to be sensible.
BORDEN: It's not going to be me.
MARY: Am I going to have to walk home from this raft?
BORDEN: Mary, I'm crazy about you.
MARY: Then try to be nice.
BORDEN: I *am* trying. *(he puts both arms about her and their lips meet)*
MARY: We'd better go back.
BORDEN: Not afraid, are you?
MARY: I'd be kind of silly if I weren't.
And she dives overboard with Borden following. They swim a few strokes and we—

FADE OUT

FADE IN

INTERIOR SAXE'S OFFICE—DAY
Medium shot—Carey and Saxe are in serious conference. Saxe's desk is piled high with stills, which they are looking at, neither of them saying a word. Only their expressions get over their reactions. Saxe looks at still of a girl and frowns, hands it to Carey, who cocks his eye admiringly. At this moment the door is thrown open and Mary's voice is heard.
MARY'S VOICE: *(excitedly)* Drop everything, boys.
Carey and Saxe look up. Mary enters scene.
CAREY: *(half rising, his lap full of stills)* What's new?
Mary swiftly extends her left hand on which is a large, square cut diamond, or emerald. The two men look at it and then back at her.
SAXE: Is it a present, or did you pay for it yourself?
MARY: It's an engagement ring.
SAXE: *(rising)* You can't do it. Who'd be foolish enough to marry a movie star?
MARY: *(laughs and turns toward door)* Lonny Borden.

CUT TO INTERIOR SAXE'S OFFICE—DAY
Medium shot—Borden stands leaning against side of doorway and smiling. Mary comes to him, and taking his hand, draws him to Saxe and Carey.
SAXE: Oh—Mr. Borden. Well, that's different. *(he starts pressing buttons)* When you going to do it?
BORDEN: In a couple of weeks. At the Little Church Around the Corner.
SAXE: Little Church nothing. At the biggest church in Beverly Hills. *(into box on his desk)* Send me all my department heads . . . send me my publicity director . . . and my fashion designer . . . and anybody that knows anything about weddings . . . *(back to Mary and Borden)* I'm going to give you the biggest wedding Hollywood has ever talked about . . . how many bridesmaids will you need? *(doesn't wait for an answer)* Not less than six . . . six big names . . . the biggest star from every studio . . .
MARY: *(interrupting)* But, Mr. Saxe, I don't know those stars . . .

SAXE: That don't matter. They'll be glad to be bridesmaids for the publicity. We'll film the wedding in color and send it out for a newsreel... we'll invite the President, the Governor and the Mayor.

CAREY: Don't overlook the Chief of Police, Saxe.

By this time three Heads of Departments enter and the Publicity Director, also the Fashion Designer.

SAXE: Gentlemen, go into an immediate conference and develop me some ideas for an outstanding wedding—something terrific.

CURTIS: For a picture, Mr. Saxe?

SAXE: No, for the newspapers. *(he turns to the Fashion Designer)* And you, Mrs. — *(he can't think of her name)*—You design me three or four Chanal Models for a wedding dress... something sensational...

FASHION DESIGNER: Yes, Mr. Saxe.

BORDEN: Pardon me, Mr. Saxe, but Miss Evans might like to select her own wedding gown.

SAXE: You don't understand, Mr. Borden. I pay Mrs. What's-Her-Name twenty-five thousand dollars a week to do nothing but think about clothes. *(turns to Publicity Director. Telephone rings)* Donald, you make immediate contact with all the newspapers, the wire services, the syndicates, the fan magazines... we'll announce this wedding at the top of our lungs... get stills of Miss Evans and Mr. Borden together— driving, playing golf, eating, swimming, doing everything... get the whole country excited... report to me your plans this afternoon... *(into box)* Miss Spiegel, get Mama on the Long Distance... Who?... Put him on... *(takes down telephone receiver)* Hello...

INTERIOR SAXE'S OFFICE—DAY
Medium shot—Mary, Carey and Borden.

MARY: *(with a little smile and extending a hand)* Aren't you even going to wish me luck?

CAREY: *(takes her hand and pats it—looks as if he were going to say something sentimental—then smiles and says flippantly)* What's the use? You know it can't last.

BORDEN: *(pleasantly touchy)* What can't last?

CAREY: *(crossly)* My liver and a movie star's marriage.

MARY: We know your liver can't last, darling.

BORDEN: Oh, he's just crabbing because you're marrying me instead of him.

42

CAREY: *(querulously)* Shut up, will you? I know I'm the face on the cutting room floor.
MARY: Nice old Carey! You stick around in case we need retakes.

INTERIOR SAXE'S OFFICE—DAY
Medium shot—Saxe seated at his desk, telephone to ear.
SAXE: Well, call me back when you get her. *(hangs up and rises)* Now— if we do this right, we get all the world talking about our wedding. We got a merger of two big industries—Motion Pictures and Society—and I tell you what'll happen—

LAP DISSOLVE

INTERIOR FIVE AND TEN CENT STORE—DAY
Medium shot—A girl is showing magazine to another clerk. Magazine has pictures of Mary and Borden and Carey, and is captioned in effect:
Insert magazine item

> *"JILTS DIRECTOR FOR POLO STAR"*
> *"The biggest wedding Hollywood has ever seen will take place next month when Mary Evans marries Lonny Borden of Santa Barbara and Oyster Bay."*

CLERK: That will put Carey back in circulation.
A customer interrupts.

LAP DISSOLVE OUT

LAP DISSOLVE IN

INTERIOR STREET CAR—DAY OR NIGHT
Medium shot—A middle-aged woman eagerly reads a newspaper over the shoulder of the man in front of her.
Insert newspaper. Headlines say:

> *"POLO STAR WINS SCREEN STAR"*
> *"Mary Evans and Lonny Borden will be married at St.*

43

Bartholomew's Church before a brilliant audience of world renowned people."

LAP DISSOLVE

INTERIOR TOWN CAR—DAY
A distinguished looking gentleman reading a paper—Winchell's column.
Insert column in paper
"Mary Evans is said to have turned down two millionaires to marry Lonny Borden. Their wedding guests will show Who's Who in Hollywood."

LAP DISSOLVE OUT

LAP DISSOLVE IN

MEDIUM SHOT—BRIDGE TABLE—DAY
Four women, talking about wedding.
FIRST WOMAN: There'll be a lot of disappointed debs when Lonny Borden marries that movie actress.
SECOND WOMAN: I don't understand it—
THIRD WOMAN: Go downtown and see her last picture and you'll understand it. She's gorgeous. What's trump?

LAP DISSOLVE

INTERIOR BOARD ROOM OF BANK—DAY
Close shot—at table. One director says in effect:
DIRECTOR: I see Lonny Borden is marrying a motion picture star. I'll bet that gives his mother a jolt.

LAP DISSOLVE OUT

LAP DISSOLVE IN

INTERIOR SAXE'S OFFICE—DAY
Saxe is still talking and the Heads are still nodding "Yes."
SAXE: And if we don't gross a million on her next picture, I'll buy everyone of you ... well, never mind, I'll forget it by that time, anyway.
They all laugh politely.

FADE OUT

FADE IN

EXTERIOR STREET—DAY
Medium shot. Five cops in a row, holding hands and being pushed from behind by a massed crowd.
Pull camera back to longer shot, showing mob gathered in front of a church, the entrance to which is roped off. A Rolls Royce waits at the curb.

CUT TO EXTERIOR STREET—DAY
Medium close shot. Muto comes up to the chauffeur and asks ingratiatingly:
MUTO: Say, Buddy, where's the wedding breakfast going to come off?
CHAUFFEUR: I don't know. Miss Evans hasn't told me.
MUTO: *(sarcastically)* Wise guy, uh?

CUT TO EXTERIOR STREET—DAY
Medium shot. A kid breaks through and starts for the church. A cop grabs him and puts him back of the rope.

CUT TO EXTERIOR STREET—DAY
Medium shot. Still Photographers jockeying for a position commanding the door of the church.

CUT TO EXTERIOR STREET—DAY
Medium close shot. A young man lifts a pocketbook from a

45

*woman's handbag and shoulders his way out of the immediate
vicinity. Woman doesn't even know it.*

CUT TO EXTERIOR STREET—DAY
*Medium close shot. A cop holding crowd back. He lets a cute little
girl get under his arm. She stands close to him.*
GIRL: *I'm* going to have a wedding like this someday.
COP: Are you in pictures?
GIRL: Oh, no. You got to be a waitress first. *(or)* Not yet. But I got a job
at the Brown Derby.

CUT TO EXTERIOR STREET—DAY
*Medium shot. A newsboy comes up the roped-off walk yelling:
"Wuxtry... Read about the War in China!" And a Voice calls:
"Who cares?" A cop starts for the boy, who runs toward the curb.*

CUT TO EXTERIOR STREET—DAY
*Medium shot. The pickpocket is standing, looking for another
haul. Newsboy dashes in, looks back, sees Cop and dashes out. Cop
enters, and at the same moment the pickpocket turns to get away.
The Cop sees him and grabs him.*
COP: Hello, Louie. I thought I'd find you here, today. Come on.
Louie meekly goes along.

CUT TO EXTERIOR STREET—DAY
*Medium shot. A man walks along edge of crowd, yelling: "Ice
Cream Cones... a nickle while they last." Another man is selling
postcards and calling: "Postcards of Mary Evans in Wedding
Dress—send them home to the folks back east."*

CUT TO EXTERIOR STREET—DAY
*Medium shot. Newsreel men and Sound Truck are lining up their
positions.*

CUT TO EXTERIOR STREET—DAY
Medium long shot. A truck drives by with music and carrying big

sign, "See Mary Evans' Latest Picture 'GIRL OF FLAME' a Julius Saxe Super Production."

CUT TO EXTERIOR STREET—DAY
Medium shot. There are several Still Photographers all set about ten feet from church door, their cameras ready. A man with a motion picture camera horns in and places his tripod. A Still Man asks: "Who you shovin'?" and suddenly, from within the church, comes the opening bars of the Wedding Recessional.

CUT TO EXTERIOR STREET—DAY
Medium shot. Six motorcycle cops lining up in front of the Rolls. Sound—wedding recessional more faintly

CUT TO EXTERIOR STREET—DAY
Medium shot. Five Cops still holding hands to prevent crowd from breaking through, but the pressure to see is too great, and the cops' hold breaks—the mob surges forward, covering the walk.

CUT TO EXTERIOR CHURCH—DAY
Medium shot. Mary and Borden come through church doors. Cameras click. A Still Photographer, Peters, has got them almost head on.
PETERS: Hey, Borden, kiss her, will you? *(Borden good-naturedly shakes his head)* Aw, come on, the public will expect it.
BORDEN: *(grinning)* No. I don't think so. *(or)* No. Not here. I'm sorry. *(he puts an arm about Mary and starts toward the curb, but the crowd surges about them)*

CUT TO EXTERIOR CHURCH—DAY
Close shot. Hands pull Mary's bouquet to pieces for souvenirs.

CUT TO EXTERIOR CHURCH—DAY
Medium close shot. Somebody with a jack knife cuts a piece of Mary's veil. Women tear more pieces of her veil for souvenirs. Mary is a bit frightened. A cop is trying to hold people off. Suddenly Borden puts his arm around Mary, turns toward the

47

church, and roughly shoulders everybody out of the way. Talk is ad lib in these mob shots.

AD LIB: *(from crowd)* Will you give me an autograph, Miss Evans? . . . Please sign my book, Mr. Borden . . .

A COP: *(yells)* Stand back there . . . Make room, please . . .

CUT TO EXTERIOR CHURCH—DAY
Medium shot. Borden is getting Mary through the crowd back into the church. Saxe and Carey are in the doorway of the church.

CUT TO INTERIOR FOYER OF CHURCH—DAY
Medium shot (traveling). Borden brings Mary through the doors. Carey grasps Borden's arm.

CAREY: Come on. This way. In here.
He leads them to a door which opens into a small room off the foyer. Saxe trots along with them. Wedding party is coming from church into foyer.

CUT TO INTERIOR SMALL ROOM—DAY
Medium shot. Carey brings Mary and Borden into room, followed by Saxe.

CAREY: Close the door. *(Saxe does so)* Your wedding is certainly a riot.

SAXE: What did I tell you. No wedding was ever like it. It breaks all the house records for this church. It's terrific.

MARY: *(almost hysterical)* How are we going to get away?

BORDEN: Do churches have back doors?

CAREY: *(holding door closed as someone tries to push inside)* You better tell 'em the bad news, Saxie.

SAXE: Not here, Carey.

MARY: *(quickly)* What bad news?

SAXE: Well, I didn't want to tell you until the last minute, but I got to ask you, Mary, to postpone your honeymoon.

BORDEN: Postpone . . . Why?

SAXE: Well, yesterday we looked at Mary's last picture. And it's perfect! But we got to have some retakes.

MARY: Couldn't they wait till I get back?

SAXE: *(as if talking to a child)* Release dates don't wait on honeymoons, my dear. There, you're disappointed, but it'll only be a week, maybe two weeks. You do this for me and some day I do something nice for you, maybe.

MARY: *(looks at Borden appealingly)* D'you mind, dear?

BORDEN: *(smiling down at her)* Of course, but it can't be helped, can it?

SAXE: *(bustling)* That's the spirit, Lonny. I go now and see about a back door.

CAREY: I'll fix it. Wait here.

> *They both go out. Left alone together, Borden sweeps Mary into his arms.*

MARY: Lonny, I think I'm going to cry.

BORDEN: Darling.

> *Their lips meet in a long kiss.*

CUT TO INTERIOR SMALL ROOM—DAY

Close shot. Peters, the photographer, appears in the window with his camera. Maybe this is a stained-glass window with a head of the Christ just over the portion that Peters opens to get his camera inside.

CUT TO INTERIOR SMALL ROOM—DAY

Medium shot. Mary and Borden still hold kiss. There is a flashlight. Peter's camera clicks, and Mary and Borden break away and look toward window.

PETERS: Thanks, folks. That was swell.

Mary and Borden stand facing him as he disappears.

FADE OUT

FADE IN

Insert of magazine.

> *Photograph of Mary and Borden kissing, captioned in effect:*
> *"SAMPLING SCREEN'S MOST FAMOUS LIPS"*
> *or*
> *"THEIR FIRST MARRIED KISS"*
> *A man's hand is holding the magazine.*

49

INTERIOR STAGE—NIGHT
Medium close shot. Borden is looking at the magazine with the photograph. Disgusted he throws it aside. Over this shot can be heard the voice of Mary singing the Belle Baker song in French "J'ai deux amis." Borden looks at his watch.
Insert watch showing 11:35.

INTERIOR STAGE—NIGHT
Medium shot. We see that Borden is on the sidelines watching while Carey is directing Mary and several tables of bald headed men in a scene. Mary is wearing as few clothes as possible and is in the act of kissing the bald heads.
MARY: *(sings) (Kisses another bald head)*
BALD HEAD: *(fatuously—closing his eyes)* Do that again.
She kisses his bald head again—a peck. Looks off at Borden and throws him a kiss with one finger.
CAREY: *(Long suffering)* No...no...if you'd forget about your husband over there, you might do this scene as if you meant it—you're treating them like a bunch of landlords—
MARY: *(amiably)* Well, you show me...
She walks over to Borden and sits down in a vacant chair beside him.

INTERIOR STAGE—NIGHT
Medium close shot Mary puts her hand on Borden's which rests on the arm of his chair.
MARY: I'm awfully sorry you've had to wait around so late, darling...
BORDEN: What do they mean saying you'd be through by eight o'clock? It's nearly midnight. Who in thunder is waiting for this picture anyway?
MARY: My public...don't be absurd.
She has picked up the magazine Borden threw aside and now opens it carelessly. Sees something that interests her.
Insert photograph of Mary and Borden kissing.
Mary shows it to Borden.
MARY: *(continued) (pleased)* Did you see us in Photoplay, darling? We're their feature article.
BORDEN: *(shortly)* Yes. Even our kisses are public property.

Mary looks up surprised at his annoyance. She is about to speak but is interrupted by Carey's voice.

CAREY'S VOICE: Miss Evans, if you please.
Mary looks up hastily.

INTERIOR STAGE—NIGHT
Medium shot. Carey gives her a look and then repeats the business she just did with Bald Head.

CAREY: *(continued) (imitating Mary) (sings song)*
BALD HEAD: *(fatuously, closing eyes)* Do that again.
Carey gives Bald Head a lingering kiss and then looks over toward Mary.

INTERIOR STAGE—NIGHT
Close shot. Mary is looking apologetically at Borden as he tears up two theater tickets. Maybe there are tears in her eyes. Borden is evidently angry.

INTERIOR STAGE—NIGHT
Medium close shot. Carey, annoyed because she is paying no attention, calls to Mary.

CAREY: Say, d'you think I'm doing this because I like it?

INTERIOR STAGE—NIGHT
Medium shot. Mary turns from Borden, and rises. Hurries toward Carey.

BORDEN: *(restrained anger)* Just who you talking to, Carey?
CAREY: I'm talking to the star of this opus who's supposed to be an actress...
BORDEN: The kind of horseplay you're doing doesn't call for acting.
CAREY: Of course you know outsiders aren't allowed on the set. Suppose you let me direct Miss Evans and you be Mr. Evans (or) you be her husband.
MARY: That's all for tonight, Max. *(she walks off in a huff)*

FADE OUT

51

FADE IN

EXTERIOR TERRACE—DAY

*Close up. The hand of a colored maid, with a lot of bracelets on it,
holds a glass pitcher from which she is pouring something into five
tall glasses on a tray. Over this shot we hear voices.*

SAXE'S VOICE: You writers should be able to tell your story in fifty
words. If you can't tell it in fifty words, it ain't a good story.

CAREY'S VOICE: Who said this was a good story? You bought it, didn't
you, Saxie?

SAXE'S VOICE: The whole story of Creation was written in three
hundred words in the Book of Genesis.

CAREY'S VOICE: There's a guy you ought to sign up.

> *Pull camera back to medium shot. We now see Mary, Carey,
> Borden, Saxe and a writer seated about a low table, where the
> colored maid finishes pouring the drinks. She is enormous and
> wears a uniform with a cap, and a lot of bracelets. Her slippers are
> cut out for enlarged joints. She goes into the house. This terrace
> opens off the living room and is furnished with wicker. The
> swimming pool is nearby. Borden doesn't enter into the contro-
> versy. He passes the others their drinks. Carey is in bathing suit
> with bathrobe. Maybe Saxe is, too.*

WRITER: *(to Mary)* Miss Evans, how do *you* like the story?

MARY: Well, I don't think I ought to be killed in the fourth reel.

SAXE: She's right, Grover. She's the star. She can't die in the fourth reel.

WRITER: But the big scene between the husband and the lover over her
grave can only happen if she's dead.

CAREY: Well, cut out the big scene. I'll put in a chase.

MARY: Do we have to do this story, Mr. Saxe?

SAXE: What's wrong with it?

MARY: There's a baby in it. Do I have to have a baby in every picture I'm
in?

WRITER: But this baby's different, Miss Evans. You get married first.

SAXE: Wait a minute. I got an idea. We'll throw the whole thing out the
window. I got a story of my own. It's my own brainchild. I had it in the
back of my head for fifteen years. It probably won't make a dime, but it's
an artistic triumph. It's about an old general. In Russia. *(He demon-*

52

strates as he talks) It's the night of the grand court ball. Splashes of color. Music. Jewels. Throbbing pulses. They are dancing a minuet. The old general is stooped and he carries a long cane as he dances with the duchess. Nobody would know he was the famous general of all Russia. Then suddenly a messenger throws open the door. He calls out, as he holds a document. "A letter from the czarina." The music stops. The general reads the letter. He takes his cane like a sword. He is not stooped now. He is the great general who is left behind ... I forgot to tell you ... because he is too old. I told the ending first, it was too dramatic. Never mind. He takes his cane and gives orders. "You go to Greece." "You take charge of the Turkish front." "You do this" and "You do that." How does it sound so far?

MARY: What part do I play? The old general?

SAXE: *(deflated)* No. The old general's mistress.

MARY: Then I won't have to have any babies.

SAXE: Yes, you're going to have a young lover.

WRITER: But Mr. Saxe, the public won't stand for costume plays.

SAXE: What do you know about the public? You've been in Hollywood too long.

WRITER: That's right. I've been here six weeks.

SAXE: Well, why don't we make it a modern Soviet picture.

WRITER: Well, what would we do about the czarina?

SAXE: She will be a female Rasputin.

MARY: Now that you've got that out of your system, can we go back to our original story?

SAXE *(resignedly):* Yes. Where were we?

MARY: I like the mythical kingdom story much better, Mr. Saxe. What d'you think, Max?

CAREY: I refuse to direct either one.

SAXE: *(mad) You* refuse. You should refuse to direct *any* story. You're lucky to get a *chance* to direct a Julius Saxe Super Production.

CAREY: If you didn't have me, you wouldn't be *making* super productions. Why don't you have somebody read these stories to you before you buy 'em?

SAXE: I can read. I can read. This is a *great* story ... It cost a lot of money ... I know a good story ... I been making smash hits for fifteen years ...

CAREY: Oh, you'd still be making custard pie pictures if it weren't for me.
MARY: Maybe we should be making custard pie pictures...
CAREY: And now you want to do a mythical kingdom...If you do another mythical kingdom you'll be a mythical producer...and you can either throw this story in your ash can, or get another boob to direct it.
SAXE: I don't know any other boob. *(Carey rises)* Where you going? You stay here and settle this picture.
CAREY: It's settled. I won't make it.
MARY: Now that that's attended to, let's decide on the story.

EXTERIOR TERRACE—DAY
Medium close shot—Borden is sitting looking at the men. His expression is one of bored displeasure. Over this shot we hear their voices arguing full tilt, all talking at once.
SAXE'S VOICE: All right, you don't make it. I get a good director.
WRITER'S VOICE: I tell you, this is a good story. I ought to know—I've had five Broadway successes.
CAREY'S VOICE: I won't make another Mythical Kingdom picture for anybody.
MARY'S VOICE: Louder, gentlemen. The neighbors can't hear you!
WRITER'S VOICE: What do you directors know about stories?
CAREY'S VOICE: A lot that you writers can't seem to learn.
SAXE'S VOICE: Is this a business or not? Am I a producer or do you hire me?
As this dogfight proceeds, Borden, with a look, rises and, taking his drink and a magazine, goes into the house. Mary, who has been watching with keen interest the three men arguing, now turns and sees Borden disappearing. She realizes he is annoyed, looks quickly at the three men and rises.

EXTERIOR TERRACE—DAY
Medium shot—Mary tries to interrupt the row and finally gets Carey's attention. He stops talking. As he does so, the writer stops.
SAXE: And I'm asking you—who pays your salary, huh?
CAREY: *(belligerently)* Wall Street.

And he starts to move away, but Saxe catches the lapels of his bathrobe and holds him.

SAXE: You're clever, huh? You have no ability, but a lot of wit. I have plenty of ability and no wit and you're going to stay right here till I think of an answer.

Mary, with a gesture of comic despair, turns and goes into the house.

CAREY: Sorry, Saxe, but I can't stay awake that long. *(and he walks off toward pool)*

EXTERIOR GARDEN—DAY
Medium shot—Bonita meets Carey as he approaches the pool.

BONITA: Oh, Mr. Carey, all mah friends think I'se got screen talent. Ah want to show you all something. Now you listen.

And she sings "Lover for Sale." Carey falls into the pool.

CUT TO INTERIOR LIVING ROOM—DAY
Full shot—Borden is stretched out on a davenport, reading a magazine. Mary enters and comes to him.

INTERIOR LIVING ROOM—DAY
Medium close shot

BORDEN: Is the dogfight over?

MARY: *(smiling)* Aren't they funny?

BORDEN: *(with a look—and without smiling)* Funny?

Mary straightens a picture.

MARY: Does that look all right?

BORDEN: *(Looks back at it—then, with a grin)* Why not try it upside ·down?

MARY: *(with a quick look at him)* You don't like the pictures in this house, do you?

BORDEN: Well, the lady that furnished this place was no connoisseur of art.

MARY: *(looking about a little wistfully)* I guess you're right. I thought it was gorgeous when I rented it. *(she goes and picks up a book and sits down)*

BORDEN *(carelessly)* It's all right, darling. What are you reading?

55

MARY: *(grimly—determined)* Emily Post. She tells you how to do everything...what forks to use and how to speak to the Prince of Wales...I'm learning the darn thing by heart.

BORDEN: *(laughing)* You funny kid! You don't have to bother with that stuff. You'll get along all right. Just be yourself.

MARY: But there's too much I don't know, Lonny.

BORDEN: *(puts down magazine—speaks teasingly)* What don't you know?

MARY: Well, this house, I thought it was all right. You think it's all wrong.

BORDEN: No I don't, honey, but you wait till our new one is finished.

MARY: And you don't approve of Bonita, even in her new uniforms... now, do you?

BORDEN: Well...

MARY: I know. Shall we get a butler?

BORDEN: *(picking up magazine again)* Not unless you want one, dear. After all, who's going to see her except Saxe and Carey and people from the studio?

MARY:: *(with a sudden flash in her eye)* And they don't count, you think?

BORDEN: *(carelessly)* Well, you must admit, they're not exactly fastidious about such things.

MARY: *(strained—rises)* Perhaps not, but they're my *friends*, Lonny. You needn't be so snooty about them.

BORDEN: Gosh! I didn't mean to be snooty, Mary. Only, honestly, you can do business with them, but do you have to make intimate *friends* of them.

MARY: No, I don't have to. I make friends of them because I *like* them. They're *human* and *kind* and not so darn superior! *(she throws Emily Post down and goes quickly to her bedroom)*
Borden follows her.

INTERIOR BEDROOM—DAY
Full shot—Mary enters and going to dressing table drawer opens it and takes out a handkerchief—blows her nose lustily. Borden comes up behind her.

56

INTERIOR BEDROOM—DAY
Medium close shot—Borden puts his arms about Mary.
BORDEN: I'm sorry, honey. You were perfectly right to resent what I said about your friends.
MARY: *(turns in his arms facing him)* Lonny, don't let's quarrel about *anything* . . . I'll learn about everything—honest I will . . . you won't have to be ashamed of me . . .
BORDEN: My sweet.
> *They kiss with all the feeling Mr. Hays will permit, and the kiss holds through two knocks at the door which finally opens and Bonita fills the doorway. Mary and Borden break away.*
BONITA: Excuse me, Miss Borden, but the lady from the fan magazine is here. She says she had an appointment.
MARY: Oh, all right, Bonita. Tell her I'll be right there.
> *She starts hurriedly powdering her nose and fixing her hair. Bonita goes out.*
BORDEN: I thought we were going to play tennis with the Rineharts.
MARY: Oh, Lonny! I forgot all about it. Gee, that's too bad. I'll telephone and explain.
> *She is putting on a string of pearls and has laid out some rings and bracelets. Borden, with a little smile, and without saying a word, takes the bracelets and all the rings away. Mary "gets" his idea.*
MARY: *(continued)* All right. *(she grins)* Come on, she'll want to meet you too.
BORDEN: No—not me.
MARY: But I promised her. Come on.
> *And he lets himself be led out.*

CUT TO INTERIOR LIBRARY—DAY
Full shot—A newspaper woman is leaning over a large photograph on the table.

INTERIOR LIBRARY—DAY
Close shot—Newspaper woman is looking at photograph of Carey which bears an inscription—
Insert inscription

57

I MADE YOU WHAT YOU ARE TODAY
I HOPE YOU'RE SATISFIED
MAX

Newspaper woman makes a knowing face and turns just as Mary enters with Borden.

MARY: How d'you do, Miss DuPont? This is my husband—

MISS DUPONT: *(gushing as she rushes forward)* How d'you do, Mr. Borden. I didn't dream you were so handsome. *What* a pair of lovers! I must photograph you looking at each other just like that. *(Borden looks uncomfortable)*

MARY: Well, let's sit down, uh? *(to Borden)* Bring up that chair, will you, dear?

MISS DUPONT: *(moves to divan and sits beside Mary)* You know, Miss Evans, I'm doing a series of articles on the Love Lives of the Picture Stars. I want your Love Life for the April number.

BORDEN: You want *what?*

MISS DUPONT: I hope you won't mind answering some rather intimate questions...you have to give them authentic stuff these days you know...and my photographer will take some pictures of you both later.

MARY: *(nervously)* Sit down, Lonny. *(he sits grimly)*

MISS DUPONT: Of course I know you both married for love, but was it the thoughtful, reasoning kind, or the blind, passionate *uhn-n-n* kind of love? *(uhn-n-n is a deep explosive descriptive grunt) (she beams on them inquiringly)*

MARY: *(with a quick glance toward Borden)* Why...why...it was...

BORDEN: *(calmly)* I think it was the uh-n-n kind. *(he doesn't emphasize the grunt as much as Miss DuPont did)*

MISS DUPONT: *(checks answer—talks as she writes)* That's good. Are you planning on having a family?

MARY: *(brightly)* I hope so. Someday.

MISS DUPONT: How interesting! Do you have separate bedrooms?

MARY: No, neither of us snores. *(she smiles tenderly at Borden—he almost glares)*

MISS DUPONT: I must photograph your bedroom. Now...How far do you think a wife should go to keep a husband's love, Miss Evans?

MARY: Well, I'd go a long ways myself.

MISS DU PONT: *(beaming)* What d'you think a husband ought to do to keep his wife's love, Mr. Borden?
BORDEN: I haven't the slightest idea...s'pose *you* tell *me?*
MISS DU PONT: *(giggles)* I've never been a husband, Mr. Borden. That reminds me, have you got a photograph showing your marvelous physique?
BORDEN: *(rising)* No—but I've got my appendix upstairs in a bottle. Perhaps you'd like to photograph that. *(and he stalks out)*
MISS DU PONT: Has he gone to get it?
MARY: I don't think so.
    As she looks after Borden, worried we

FADE OUT

FADE IN

INTERIOR SAXE'S OFFICE—DAY
Medium shot. Saxe is eating his lunch off a tray. He is eating with one hand and holding manuscript with the other. Saxe turns from reading the manuscript to the dictaphone.
MISS SPIEGEL'S VOICE: Yes, Mr. Saxe.
SAXE: Have you got any news of Carey yet?
MISS SPIEGEL'S VOICE: No, Mr. Saxe.
SAXE: *(worried but irritable)* Did you call all the hospitals?
MISS SPIEGEL'S VOICE: Yes, sir.
SAXE: And the morgue?
MISS SPIEGEL'S VOICE: Yes, sir.
SAXE: *(relieved)* All right. He ain't dead anyway. *(returns to manuscript and food)*
    The next moment Mary bursts in.
MARY: May I come in, Mr. Saxe?
SAXE: Oh, hello, Mary. Sure, come in. *(he puts down manuscript)*
MARY: Mr. Saxe, the *Hollywood Mirror* says you've hired a new director to finish Max Carey's picture.
SAXE: *(quickly)* And for once, the *Hollywood Mirror* is right.
MARY: *(appealingly)* Oh, Mr. Saxe, that will break his heart.

SAXE: Well, already he has broke my heart and my pocket book. *(Mary puts her bag on his desk and sits)* I should pay a company for one week to do nothing, while Carey goes on a binge.

MARY: Where is he now?

SAXE: *(excitedly)* You ask *me* where he is? I been asking the whole world where he is for one week. Nobody knows where he is, and I don't care.

MARY: I'll find him... I'll bring him back. *(she rises and picks up her bag)*

SAXE: It won't do you no good, Mary. This time I fired him for good, and I mean it.

MARY: *(appealingly)* But, Mr. Saxe, if Max ever needed help, it's right now. He's been a great director... he can be again... if you kick him out now, it'll finish him.

SAXE: And if I don't, it'll finish me. I've let sentiment interfere with good sense too long, Mary. Besides, nobody knows where he is anyway, and the picture has got to go on.

MARY: I'll find him. *(she starts for the door)*

SAXE: *(calls after her)* If he's in jail, I'll bail him out, but I won't give him a job, I'm tellin' you.

> *Mary is out the door and Saxe goes on with his eating, but it doesn't taste good, and he throws down his napkin and begins searching fussily for a cigar which he finds and viciously bites.*

FADE OUT

FADE IN

INTERIOR BEDROOM—NIGHT
Insert column in newspaper or trade paper

> *Hollywood is laying bets on where a certain blonde star will find her errant director. The young lady has spent the past two days unsuccessfully combing the speakeasies and dives of Los Angeles.*

A man's hand tears the paper.
Pull camera back to medium shot. Borden is in one twin bed angrily tearing the paper he has just read. Mary is in the other bed, studying lines.

BORDEN: Filthy rag!

MARY: *(looks up)* I don't know how they find out everything I do.

BORDEN: That's their business. You're in the Hollywood spotlight. You *know*, everything about you is exaggerated and discussed in newspapers and magazines and around the studios. After all you might think of me . . . of appearances.

MARY: Appearances? Listen, Lonny, Carey's fired, and I don't want him rolling in gutters where all his fair-weather friends can see him and laugh at him.

BORDEN: He brought it on himself.

MARY: I'm never going to throw Carey down. He gave me my first break.

BORDEN: But you're throwing me down. No privacy—no home life. Couldn't you arrange to keep your business at the studio and not drag it home?

MARY: Maybe it would be a good idea if I stayed at the studio myself.

BORDEN: Don't be nasty.

MARY: I'm not nasty—I'm tired of arguing. Sometimes I think life is just one great big argument.

BORDEN: Mary, I was just thinking . . .

There is heard from off a magnificent yodel. Mary and Borden listen. The yodel is repeated.

BORDEN: *(puzzled)* What's that?

MARY: It's Carey.

CUT TO EXTERIOR MARY'S HOME—THE LAWN—NIGHT

Carey is shown, ginned up, and moving through the grounds. He pauses beside a statue of a nude woman, whose marble posterior is at level of Carey's face. He scratches a match on the marble posterior, then looks at the statue. He bows to the statue.

CAREY: *(to statue)* I thought you had pants on. *(he cups his mouth with his palm and exits a masterly yodel)* Ade-lay-a-hoo! Ho, landlord!

CUT TO INTERIOR MARY'S BEDROOM—NIGHT

Mary and Borden. Borden is up and beside the window.

BORDEN: *(to Carey, off)* Pipe down, old man. We want to sleep.

MARY: That's not way to handle him.

CAREY: *(off-scene)* Let a little sunshine in. *(yodels again)*
  Shot of Borden, disgusted.

CUT TO EXTERIOR HOME—THE GROUNDS—NIGHT
Close shot of Carey. He is in a flower bed beneath Mary's lighted window. He is picking up a newspaper and is crumpling it. He puts crumpled paper to ground and reaches for his matches. He begins striking matches, but they go out.
Shot of Borden leaning from window. Mary pops her head out.
BORDEN: What do you think this is?
CAREY: *(singing)* On the mountain top, I became a flop. Ado-lay-eee. Ad-a-lay-o-hoo.
MARY: Be a good boy, Max, and go on home.
CAREY: I got something important to tell you.
MARY: Well, what is it?
CAREY: Nothing.
BORDEN: Now go on home, old man.
CAREY: *(striking matches on wall)* Don't call me an old man, or I'll burn your house down. I think I'll burn it down anyway. Are you going to let me in?

CUT TO INTERIOR MARY'S LIVING ROOM—NIGHT
Bonita in a negligee with swansdown, as she opens front door—Carey staggering up to the door.
MARY: *(off scene—calling)* Bonita, put Mr. Carey to bed.
BONITA: Yes, ma'am. Come in, Mr. Carey.
  Bonita ushers Carey in.

FADE OUT

FADE IN

INTERIOR MARY'S BEDROOM—NIGHT
Mary and Borden are in bed—lights are out—only the moonlight flooding in through the window. There is a knock heard at the door.
BORDEN: Who is it?

CAREY: *(opens the door and enters)* Me ... am I interrupting anything? *(sees he isn't and ambles toward beds)* I've been doing a lot of thinking— and I can't think any more. Where's your liquor?

BORDEN: This isn't a night club.

MARY: Be a good boy, Max, and go to bed.

CAREY: I'm not sleepy.

BORDEN: *(getting very sore)* Would you do me a favor and go home.

CAREY: *(ignoring Borden, goes over and seats himself on the edge of Mary's bed)* Mary, would you two mind if I'd be serious for a little while.

MARY: Now go on to bed, Max.

CAREY: No, I have something of interest to say to both of you.

BORDEN: *(gets out of bed and puts on dressing gown—to Carey)* Maybe you'd be more comfortable if you come over and get into *this* bed.

MARY: Lonny, this is going just a little bit too far.

CAREY: I don't blame him a bit. He doesn't understand people like us.

BORDEN: And doesn't want to.

CAREY: *(interrupting)* Will you excuse us while we talk? I want to give Mary some good advice. You can listen if you want to—it might do you some good.

> Borden picks up his clothes and starts out of scene.

MARY: Where are you going?

BORDEN: As far away from Hollywood and all its inmates as I can.

CAREY: Let him go ... he'll come back!

MARY: I don't care whether he comes back or not.

BORDEN: *(enters with trousers and shirt on. Finishes tying tie)* I'm not coming back. I'm fed up on this kind of living. I should have known better in the first place ... we don't live in the same worlds.

MARY: *(furiously)* That's right. I live in a world where people are human beings—not stuffed shirts.

BORDEN: You live in a world where people are vulgar and cheap without knowing it—and if you weren't vulgar and cheap yourself, you couldn't stand it.

MARY: All right, if that's the way you feel get out! *GET OUT! GET OUT!!!* *(he goes and Mary turns to Carey)* and you get out too ... and leave me alone ... *GET OUT!*

> Carey goes out. Mary then breaks into hysterical weeping.

FADE OUT

63

FADE IN
Insert newspaper headlines in effect:

"LONNY BORDEN ESTABLISHES
RESIDENCE IN RENO."

LAP DISSOLVE
Insert newspaper headlines in effect:

"MARY EVANS DENIES DIVORCE."

LAP DISSOLVE
Insert newspaper headlines in effect:

"POLO STAR SUES FILM STAR."

LAP DISSOLVE

EXTERIOR RANCH—NIGHT
Long shot—showing in the distance a group of small buildings, and around one of them is a circle of light.

LAP DISSOLVE

EXTERIOR RANCH—NIGHT
Medium shot—Cameras are turning on a scene of Mary in the rain outside a house or whatever building is available. We don't need dialogue for this scene. Mary comes to a window and peers inside. There is a sound of a motor car stopping and Mary turns, sees car and ducks behind some bushes. Leading man can be brought in if desired.
DIRECTOR: Cut. O.K. for sound?
VOICE: O.K. for sound.
ASSISTANT DIRECTOR: Mark it.
Mary walks out of a scene and steps out of character.

64

EXTERIOR RANCH—NIGHT

Medium close shot—Mary comes to a heater and her maid wraps a warm blanket around her. Mary is shivering. Carey is fixing coffee and hands Mary a steaming cup.

MARY: After this, my rain is going to be heated.

CAREY: Here's some that's boiling, only they call it coffee.

At this moment the Assistant Director enters.

ASSISTANT DIRECTOR: Here are your lines for the next scene, Miss Evans.

MARY: Thanks, Jimmie.

CAREY: *(turns around)* How are you, Jimmie?

ASSISTANT DIRECTOR: Hello, Mr. Carey. Awfully good to see you again. *(quietly)* Wish you were directing this picture.

CAREY: He's doing a better job than I could. Have some coffee?

CUT TO EXTERIOR RANCH—NIGHT

Medium shot—Saxe's car drives up close to set and stops. Saxe gets out and starts toward Mary.

EXTERIOR RANCH—NIGHT

Medium shot—Mary, Carey and Assistant Director are drinking coffee. Assistant puts his cup down and turns to go.

ASSISTANT DIRECTOR: Thanks.

Saxe enters scene.

SAXE: *(shouts)* What's holding this up? What's keeping the film from going through the camera? *(to Mary)* What are you doing standing here in soaked clothes? *(to assistant)* What's the meaning of this? Don't you realize we have a million dollar investment in Miss Evans? And here she is risking her life with pneumonia—America's pal! Get her some dry clothes.

ASSISTANT DIRECTOR: Sure, Mr. Saxe. But you know, it's just one of those scenes.

SAXE: *(turns to Carey)* Oh, good evening, Maximilian.

CAREY: Bon Soir, Monsieur La Saxe.

SAXE: How long has it been since you've had a drink?

CAREY: Oh, about six weeks.

SAXE: Six weeks?

65

CAREY: Well, about four.

SAXE: Not a drop in four weeks?

CAREY: Well, not for a couple of days except for a little wine tonic. I just bottled a fresh batch of homebrew and it's swell. *(belches)* Okay for sound.

CUT TO EXTERIOR RANCH—NIGHT
Medium shot. A messenger boy is just arriving on a motorcycle. He stops and gets off.

EXTERIOR RANCH—NIGHT
Medium shot—The messenger boy enters and gives Mary a telegram.

MESSENGER: Miss Evans?

MARY: Yes.
She takes telegram while her maid signs and pays the boy who leaves. Mary reads:
Insert telegram

"Dear Mary. You will be glad to know that I am no longer Mr. Mary Evans. You are now free, white and twenty-one. Divorce was granted today.
Larry."

EXTERIOR RANCH—NIGHT
Close up—Mary finishes reading the telegram and tries not to give way.

ASSISTANT DIRECTOR'S VOICE: All right Miss Evans for the next scene if you're ready.
Mary makes a desperate effort to hang onto herself, tries to smile as she says—

MARY: All right. I'm . . . ready . . .
But she can't do it. She is going to break. She turns toward Saxe.

EXTERIOR RANCH—NIGHT
Medium close shot. Mary takes a few steps and reaches Saxe.

66

SAXE: *(seeing her face)* Why, Mary, what's the matter, darling?
Without a word she hands him the wire, which he reads and then looks at her.
SAXE: *(continued) (determined to cheer her)* Well, that's fine! He never did understand you. It's better this way. You should be happy.
MARY: *(hysterically)* Happy? Sure I'm happy. Why shouldn't I be? I'm going to have a baby in September. *(she breaks completely)*
Saxe opens his arms and she goes into them, weeping.
SAXE: *(petting her as he would a child)* There, there, it'll be a blessing!

FADE OUT
It is two and a half years later.

FADE IN

EXTERIOR STREET—DAY
Medium close shot (Traveling). A rubberneck wagon with a dozen or more tourists is making the rounds of the stars' homes in Beverly Hills.
BARKER: *(with megaphone)* Ladies and Gentlemen, you are seeing the homes of all the outstanding stars of Cinemaland. We are now coming to—not the largest, but one of the most charming little estates in Beverly Hills. I refer to the home of America's Pal, Miss Mary Evans—on your right.
Everybody turns to look eagerly.
AD LIB: Oh, isn't it lovely? . . . Oh, Mary Evans is my favorite star! . . . I got a picture of Mary Evans . . .

CUT TO EXTERIOR MARY'S NEW HOME—DAY
Long shot—showing a lovely house in beautiful, well-kept grounds. Something with fine lines architecturally dignified and in excellent taste.
BARKER'S VOICE: *(over scene)* This house was two years in the building, and received first prize from the California Architectural Society. It is said the interior is a model of taste, in decoration and furnishing. Miss Evans had a special nursery built at a cost of . . . *(dies out, giving the impression that the wagon goes on)*

LAP DISSOLVE OUT

67

LAP DISSOLVE IN

INTERIOR LIVING ROOM OF MARY'S NEW HOME—DAY
Medium close shot (Traveling). Mary is holding the hand of a young man of two, and together they are looking for something.
MARY: Now where d'you suppose the bunny would leave those Easter eggs—
BOBBIE: There, Mom... there! *(the youngster makes a dive into the corner of the davenport where there is a little basket of colored eggs)*
MARY: Oh, you found them! Maybe there are more. Let's look over here.

INTERIOR LIVING ROOM OF MARY'S NEW HOME—DAY
Longer shot—showing Saxe watching Mary and Bobbie hunt for Easter eggs.
SAXE: What a cute little fella he's getting to be. We soon have a new screen lover.
Nurse enters to get baby.

INTERIOR LIVING ROOM OF MARY'S NEW HOME—DAY
Medium shot—Mary adroitly leads baby to look under a chair or a table or whatever.
MARY: I wonder if a bunny could get under here?
BOBBIE: *(excitedly)* Yes... yes... I see 'em! *(he dives in and brings out more eggs)*
While the baby is dragging out the eggs, a butler approaches Mary. He has a live white rabbit in a wooden cage effect. Attached to the cage is an envelope.
BUTLER: This just came for Bobbie, Miss Evans.
MARY: Oh, how cunning! *(she quickly opens envelope and takes out a note)* Thank you, Martin.
Martin puts cage on the table and goes out.
Mary reads note:
Insert

Dear Mary—
Would you mind if the young man had an Easter gift from
the old man?
                    Lonny
            (or)
Do you mind if I send an Easter gift to our son?
                    Lonny
Mary smiles, takes the rabbit from the cage, and looks at it with
unusual tenderness. She holds it close to her cheek.
BOBBIE'S VOICE: Bunny, Mom! Bunny!
Mary is reminded that the gift is for her son, and turns quickly.
MARY: Here's your bunny, son—a *beautiful* birthday present from your
daddy.
Bobbie takes bunny and hugs it.
SAXE: *(with a look at Mary)* Ah! From his daddy. Is Lonny in town,
Mary?
MARY: No.
SAXE: I read in the paper he is going to play polo in Del Monte next
month.
MARY: *(elaborately careless)* Yes. I understand he's engaged to a girl
there.
SAXE: I'll bet he would like you should take him back? Why don't you?
MARY: *(with a pat on his shoulder and a smile)* Stop writing scenarios,
Saxie. *(she turns to the baby, and the next moment the butler re-enters)*
BUTLER: There's someone on the telephone, Miss Evans, who says he's
James, Mr. Carey's chauffeur. He said you'd remember him...
MARY: *(to Saxe)* James! I wonder what he wants. I'll be right back. *(she
goes)*

CUT TO INTERIOR HALL—MARY'S NEW HOME—DAY
Full shot—showing spacious beautiful hall and stairway. Mary
enters and goes to telephone.

INTERIOR HALL—MARY'S NEW HOME—DAY
Close shot—Mary at telephone.
MARY: *(in phone)* Hello...yes, James, how are you?

CUT TO INTERIOR DRUG STORE—DAY
Close shot. James is talking on telephone. He wears a taxi-driver's uniform.
JAMES: *(in phone)* Ah accidentally run across Mr. Carey yesterday, and he's in pretty bad shape, Miss Evans... Ah think he needs a doctor...

CUT TO INTERIOR HALL—MARY'S NEW HOME—DAY
Medium close shot—Mary at telephone.
MARY: *(in phone)* I'm glad you called me, James. Meet me at the Studio right away. We'll go and get him... Goodbye! *(she hangs up and turns thoughtfully to go out)*

FADE OUT

FADE IN

EXTERIOR OF A DUMP—DAY
Medium long shot—Mary, driven by her own chauffeur with James in the front seat beside him, arrives at the curb. Mary gets out and goes in, followed by James.

INTERIOR DUMP—HALLWAY—DAY
Medium shot. Mary enters, hurries along hallway to a door which she opens.

INTERIOR BACK ROOM—DUMP—DAY
Full shot, Mary pushes open the door and enters. At a table, in the center of the room, a floosie in a kimono is playing solitaire, a drink in front of her. On a couch nearby lies Carey, dead to the world. Mary crosses to him quickly. Floosie looks up and sees her.
FLOOSIE: *(sourly)* Well, why don't you come in? Don't bother to knock.
MARY: *(over her shoulder as she bends over Carey)* I'm a friend of Mr. Carey's.
FLOOSIE: *(blinking)* So'm I. He's drunker'n a goat.

INTERIOR BACK ROOM—DUMP—DAY
Close shot. Mary leans over Carey, who is dirty and unshaven, and shakes him.

70

MARY: Max! Max!

CAREY: *(opens one eye)* Whassamatter? Who you jigglin'?

MARY: It's Mary. I've come to take you home, Max.

CAREY: *(gets good look at her—rises on elbow)* Thass right! 'Tis Mary... Who told you I was here?

MARY: *(gently)* Never mind. I've been looking for you for months. Come on. *(she tries to help him get to his feet)*

CAREY: *(turns and looks at her with a little smile of tenderness and gratitude, then suddenly frowns)* You shouldn't come to a place like this, Mary... Got to get you out of here. *(he gets to his feet)*

> INTERIOR BACK ROOM—DUMP—DAY
> *Medium shot. Carey tries to stand erect, takes a step and puts a hand over his heart, and catches his breath. A spasm of pain crosses his face.*

MARY: *(concerned—taking his arm)* You're ill, Max. You must see a doctor.

CAREY: *(pain has passed and he breathes freely again)* Not me. A doctor'll tell me I drink too much... *(he smiles down at her)*

MARY: *(smiles back)* Well, you can always argue the point with him. *(she gently propels him forward)*

CAREY: *(seriously)* That's right, I can.

> *Carey walks with difficulty. Mary motions James with her head to come. James, who is standing in the doorway, now approaches and takes Carey's other arm. Carey sees him.*

CAREY: *(continued)* Oh, there's Jimmy... Hello, James... Anything new?...

JAMES: Hello, Mr. Carey! Glad to see you, sir.

CAREY: I never realized how much I've missed you two.

> *By this time they are through the door, and we—*

> LAP DISSOLVE OUT

> LAP DISSOLVE IN

> INTERIOR HALLWAY—MARY'S NEW HOME—DAY
> *Full shot. Butler opens the door, and Mary and James bring Carey inside. Butler closes door.*

71

MARY: Martin, will you please show James the way to the guest room? Mr. Carey is ill, and James will put him to bed.

MARTIN: Yes, Miss Evans. *(to James)* Will you come this way? May I help?

CAREY: *(to butler)* Thanks, old man, I'm doing fine.

But, on the second step of the stairs, he misses his footing, and James has all he can do to hold him up. Butler helps. Mary watches, distressed.

FADE OUT

FADE IN

INTERIOR GUEST ROOM—DAY
Full shot—Carey is in bed, a nurse is looking at a chart which hangs on the wall at one side of the bed. A doctor is writing a prescription at the other side. Mary is seated on the side of the bed, holding Carey's hand.

DOCTOR: You're doing me proud, Mr. Carey. In another week or ten days, you'll be able to go back to work.

CAREY: *(with a touch of bitterness)* Work and I haven't been on speaking terms for a couple of years, Doctor.

MARY: *(loyally)* And whose fault is that? You just wait till the studios know you'll accept a picture.

CAREY: *(with a grateful, amused smile at Mary and a pat of his hand)* O.K. I'll wait.

DOCTOR: And now, you get a little nap, uh? *(Mary gets up to go)*

CAREY: And if I can't sleep, I'll cry for my bottle.

MARY: If you can't sleep, you count your new red corpuscles as they multiply.

She fixes the bedclothes and goes out with the doctor. The nurse lowers the shades and prepares to follow.

CUT TO INTERIOR MARY'S LIVING ROOM—DAY
Medium shot—Saxe is standing reading a letter which he puts in his pocket as Mary enters.

MARY: Hello, Saxie!

72

SAXE: *(as they move toward divan)* Hello Mary! How is Carey, today?
MARY: Much better. The doctor says he'll be able to go to work in a week or so.
SAXE: *(genuinely pleased)* Oh! That's fine. You've given him the best care, Mary ... you've been a good friend ... but I'll be glad when he's out of your house.
MARY: *(on the defensive)* I s'pose you've heard some gossip.
SAXE: Why wouldn't there be gossip, my dear ... when a beautiful young divorcee installs a man in her home.
MARY: Even when he's as sick as Max was?
SAXE: A man is a man even if he *is* sick, and besides, Max is almost well, now. *(cajolingly)* You better let him go somewhere else. Be sensible.
MARY: All right. Max will be moved out of this house the day you promise to give him a job.
SAXE: But Mary ... he's not a good director any more ...
MARY: Yes he is. He'll come back strong. *(pleads)* Give him a chance, Saxie. He made you a lot of money in the old days.
SAXE: But these are new days—
MARY: Let him direct my next picture. I'm willing to gamble and I've got something to lose, too. Let's give him one more chance, Saxie.
SAXIE: All right, Mary. You do four pictures next year instead of three for the same salary and I'll do it.
MARY: Four pictures it is.
SAXE: And move Carey to a hotel tomorrow.
MARY: If the doctor is willing ... *(Saxe beams—she reaches for his hand and shakes it)* Saxie, you're what America's Pal calls a Pal! *(they shake hands and laugh)*

FADE OUT

FADE IN

EXTERIOR STREET AT RANCH—DAY
Medium shot. Carey is waiting for the lights to be placed. Mary is in a chair marked with her name.
CAREY: Whenever you're ready, boys.

ELECTRICIAN: Just a minute, Mr. Carey. Move that reflector, Pete.
Pete moves the reflector a little. At this moment Saxe enters to Mary.

EXTERIOR STREET RANCH—DAY
Medium close shot. Saxe takes Mary's hand.
SAXE: Come for a little walk. I want to talk with you.
Mary rises and goes with him.

EXTERIOR STREET RANCH—DAY
Close shot. Carey sees Saxe lead Mary off the set. He watches them a moment, realizing there is something in the wind.

EXTERIOR STREET RANCH—DAY
Medium close shot. Mary and Saxe stop while Saxe tells her what's on his chest.
SAXE: I've looked at all the stuff he's shot and I tell you, Mary, it's very bad.
MARY: It didn't feel so bad while I was doing it.
SAXE: You sure he isn't drinking on the quiet?
MARY: I'm sure he hasn't touched a drop since the picture started.
SAXE: Well, then he just can't direct when he's sober. I'm going to tell him.
MARY: Wait, Saxie. Can't you let him finish it? It's only a week more. Another director couldn't possibly make much difference now.
SAXE: No, Mary. I've got New York bankers to think of. It ain't fair. I've got to let Carey go.
MARY: Then let me tell him . . . please.
SAXE: *(delighted)* All right. Go ahead. I'd have fixed him a *week* ago if I thought *you'd tell* him. *(they move toward set)*

EXTERIOR STREET RANCH—DAY
Medium shot. Mary and Saxe come to place they left Carey. He is nowhere to be seen. Mary looks about.
MARY: *(to assistant)* Where's Max?
ASSISTANT: *(uncertainly)* I don't know, Miss Evans. He just said he was retiring from pictures and walked away.

74

Mary turns and looks at Saxe.
SAXE: Smart fella! He always was a jump ahead of me. *(to assistant)* Dismiss the company. That'll be all for today. *(Mary and Saxe turn to leave)*
ASSISTANT: *(calls)* Wrap 'em up.

FADE OUT

FADE IN

INTERIOR LIVING ROOM—MARY'S NEW HOME—NIGHT
Medium shot—Mary is propped up on the davenport, studying a script, memorizing lines.
MARY: *(memorizing)* "Go back to your father and tell him I don't want his name. I can get a better one."
At this moment there is a tap on the window. Mary turns quickly and sees Carey's face peering in. The she hears him yodel. She rises and goes toward hall.

INTERIOR HALL—MARY'S NEW HOME—NIGHT
Medium shot—Mary enters and opens the door. Carey stands in doorway. He is thoroughly oiled.
CAREY: Hello, Mary! I'm drunk.
MARY: *(startled at his appearance)* Max, you look terrible! Come in. *He enters, stops, then makes a terrific effort to walk toward living room. Mary closes the door and follows him quickly.*

INTERIOR LIVING ROOM—MARY'S NEW HOME—NIGHT
Medium shot—Carey sinks onto the davenport, and Mary stis down beside him.
MARY: You're sick, Max. I'll telephone Dr. Harrison.
CAREY: No. Just give me a drink, Mary. I'll be all right...
MARY: I daren't give you anything to drink, dear. You know what the doctors said.
CAREY: But I've had some... I've had a lot and it didn't kill me... Doctors don't always know everything...
MARY: Max, why did you do it?

75

CAREY: *(with real feeling)* Because I've ruined your picture...

MARY: *(loyally)* No you haven't Max.

CAREY: I know. Saxie wanted to fire me...you wouldn't let him...

MARY: Listen, dear, you don't believe all the gossip in a studio...

CAREY: *(irrelevantly)* You're a sweet kid, Mary...but I'm onto myself...I thought it might be a fairly good picture, too.

MARY: It *is* good, Max.

CAREY: *(bitterly)* No, it isn't! It's terrible! *(he buries his face in his hands)*

MARY: If it is, it's my fault, Max. I wanted to make the story... *(or)* No matter what it is, it isn't your fault, Max. We all agreed on the story, and you've worked harder than any of us...

CAREY: *(looks up and smiles at her gratefully)* You *would* say that! How 'bout a little drink? *(desperately)* I...I *need* it, Mary.

MARY: I'll call the doctor. If he says yes, I'll give you some. *(she rises)*

CAREY: Mary, who's going to finish your picture?

MARY: *(realizing how much her answer means to him)* You are, if you'll just pull yourself out of this.

CAREY: *(wistfully)* Did Saxie say so?

MARY: Of course. He wants you to finish it. Now you hang on.... I'll be right back.

CAREY: *(catching her hand, as she turns)* Mary.

MARY: Yes, dear.

CAREY: *(from his heart)* There never *was* another girl like you...I've known it from the first time we met...You started in taking care of me...

MARY: *(with mock severity)* And I'm about through. I'm going to get you your last drink, young fella. You're going dry again from tomorrow on.

> He smiles at her, and she withdraws her hand, fixes his pillow, and, as he sinks back on it, she hurries out. Carey reaches in his pocket and pulls out a cigarette and a few matches, lights them, then his hand falls, and the lighted matches drop onto the floor.
>
> Insert close up of burning matches until they go out.
>
> Shoot death scene two ways—Once with revolver to indicate suicide.

INTERIOR HALLWAY—NIGHT
Medium shot—Mary at telephone.

MARY: *(in a low voice)* Hello, Dr. Harrison please. Miss Evans. *(waits)* Hello, Doctor... Fine, thanks... it's about Max Carey. He's off the wagon... quite a bit I'm afraid... he's here and wants a drink... I was afraid to give it to him... yes, pretty bad shape... thanks doctor. Yes. Goodbye. *(she hangs up and goes toward living room)*

INTERIOR LIVING ROOM—NIGHT
Full shot—Mary enters from hall and approaches the davenport where Carey is lying. She bends over him and it begins to dawn on her that he is dead. Suddenly she drops on her knees beside him and begins to rub his hands with her own.

MARY: Max! Max!
She realizes he is beyond her aid and a sob escapes her. She gets slowly to her feet, crying, and runs to the telephone.

INTERIOR HALL—NIGHT
Medium shot—Mary runs into scene and dials O-operator.

MARY: *(trying to control her voice)* Operator... get me the emergency hospital... quick... *(she weeps audibly as she waits)*

FADE OUT

FADE IN

INTERIOR RADIO ROOM—NIGHT
Medium shot—An Announcer is reading the midnight news broadcast. A man hands him a slip of paper.

ANNOUNCER: And the Senate is still investigating the matter. *(he glances at slip of paper)* And now ladies and gentlemen we have just received some news that will be a great shock to the Hollywood film colony. Maxmillian Carey, the well known director; was found dead under mysterious circumstances in the home of Mary Evans tonight. The two were alone in the house when the tragedy occurred. There seems to be some question as to whether the death was suicide or from natural causes. Coroner Mills has ordered an autopsy. Maxmillian Carey was the discoverer of Mary Evans and directed many of her successes. At the time of her divorce from the famous Polo Star, Lonny Borden, the name of Mr. Carey was mentioned as being the cause of the marital rift, but he was not named in the divorce suit—

INTERIOR COCOANUT GROVE—NIGHT
Full shot—Dancing, dining, music. Dancing ends. As people take their seats.

INTERIOR COCOANUT GROVE—NIGHT
Medium shot—Someone whispers to the leader of the orchestra who is broadcasting. Leader turns and announces:
LEADER: Ladies and gentlemen, there has just been an announcement over the radio that Maxmillian Carey died tonight under mysterious circumstances in the home of Mary Evans. The Coroner has ordered an autopsy to determine whether death was due to suicide or natural causes.

INTERIOR COCOANUT GROVE—NIGHT
Medium close shot—A table of four, evidently picture people.
1ST DINER: What d'you know about that? Was Max Carey living at Mary's home?
2ND DINER: Nobody'll believe it if he wasn't.

CUT TO INTERIOR COCOANUT GROVE—NIGHT
Medium close shot—Another table.
3RD DINER: D'you think he killed himself on her account?
4TH DINER: Maybe somebody killed him. Where's her divorced husband?

CUT TO INTERIOR COCOANUT GROVE—NIGHT
Medium close shot—Another table.
FIFTH DINER: What an awful thing to happen to Mary Evans.
SIXTH DINER-GIRL: Well, there goes *her* career. Julius Saxe will be needing a new pal for America. *(she gets out mirror and fixes herself)*

FADE OUT

FADE IN
Insert newspaper headline

   "Mysterious Death in Star's Home"

LAP DISSOLVE
Insert Headline

   "Mary Evans Denies Carey Romance"

LAP DISSOLVE
Insert headline

   "Star Faints At Director's Grave"

LAP DISSOLVE
Insert headline

   "Film Scandal Stirs Nation"

LAP DISSOLVE
Insert headline

   "Exhibitors Cancel Mary Evan's Films"

LAP DISSOLVE
Insert headline

   "Scandal Blasts Star's Career"

LAP DISSOLVE

EXTERIOR MARY'S NEW HOME—DAY
Medium long shot—Showing a group of reporters in a car on the driveway or wherever. Beside the front door stands two guards. A still camera man is taking pictures of the house and grounds.

EXTERIOR MARY'S NEW HOME—DAY
Medium close shot—Reporters in car marked Press.
1ST REPORTER: I wonder how long this Evans-Carey story will hog the front pages.
2ND REPORTER: Long enough to wash her up in pictures.

CUT TO EXTERIOR MARY'S NEW HOME—DAY
Medium shot—A couple of reporters climb over a wall and approach the back door and ring the bell.

EXTERIOR MARY'S NEW HOME—DAY
Medium close shot—Reporter keeps his finger on bell. Nobody opens the door but we hear the sound of steady ringing.
3RD REPORTER: They won't answer. I rang the front door bell for five hours yesterday.
  At this moment a window opens and Bonita sticks her head out.
BONITA: You reporters will have to get out. Miss Evans is not seeing anybody at all.
4TH REPORTER: Is she home?
BONITA: Ah don't know nothin' about where she is. You'll have to stay off the premises, that's all.
3RD REPORTER: You tell her she'd get a lot better break from the papers if she'd play ball.
  They go.

CUT TO EXTERIOR MARY'S NEW HOME—DAY
Medium close shot—Still man is snapping pictures.
REPORTER: That's the window of the room where it happened. Get it.
  Still man snaps it.

LAP DISSOLVE OUT

LAP DISSOLVE IN

INTERIOR LIVING ROOM—DAY
Medium shot. Mary and Saxe are in the midst of a hectic conference. Mary is pacing the floor. Saxe is seated on the edge of

the bank. The chairs, tables and floor are strewn with newspapers. The telephone bell rings in the distance almost continuously, also the doorbell. Mary stops near a window. She is at the breaking point.

MARY: *(at window)* Can't we get rid of those reporters? Can't you make them leave me alone...?

SAXE: *(soothingly)* Now, sit down Mary...be calm...they're just doing their job...

MARY: It's easy for you to be calm! People aren't whispering about you—printing lies about you...turning against you... *(she breaks a little)*...and what did I do? I brought a sick man to my house...

SAXE: *(with tender sympathy)* I know Mary and it breaks my heart too. But people don't understand relationships like yours and Carey's.

MARY: *(interrupts passionately)* I'm glad I did! I'd do it all over again! I was the only friend he had ... I only wanted to help him ... *(she begins to cry and sits resting her head on her hand, moving it from side to side as if it ached)*

SAXE: *(patting her shoulder)* Of course you did, darling, and if you were just an ordinary girl, it would have been all right. But you're a motion picture star ... you belong to the public—they make you and they break you ...

MARY: *(rising again with determination)* Well, they're not going to break me without a fight. I've worked too hard to get where I am. I'm going to tell them *my* side ...

SAXE: *(trying to cheer her)* That's a good idea. We will invite all the newspaper boys to my office and you will make a statement ...

MARY: *(eagerly)* D'you think that will do any good Saxe?

SAXE: Sure it will do good. The public doesn't want to be unjust, Mary. We'll try it anyway.

MARY: *(hopefully)* You think they'll believe I'm telling the truth?

SAXE: *(consolingly)* Of course they will. And in a few months, it will all be forgotten.

MARY: *(with a touch of bitterness)* In a few months Mary Evans will be forgotten. America will have another pal.

SAXE: Nobody will ever take your place, darling.

MARY: *(patting his hand)* You're just being sweet ... but I won't give up ... it isn't just a career I'm thinking about ... *(she tries not to break)*

I've got a son, Saxie . . . I want to clear my name for his sake . . . don't you see, dear . . . *(she catches hold of both his arms)* I've *got* to! I've *got* to fight this thing, for Jackie's sake!

At this moment the butler enters with a note which he hands to Mary.

BUTLER: A reporter sent this in, Miss Evans.

He goes out. Mary opens note with nervous fingers.

Insert pencil scrawl—

> *Is it true that Lonny Borden is on his way here to get possession of his son?*

Mary looks up terrfied.

MARY: Saxie, I've got to get away . . .

SAXE: *(quickly)* What is it?

MARY: *(shows him paper—she is deadly afraid. He is reading it as she speaks)* I've got to get Jackie away to Europe where nobody can find us . . . *(she is thinking frantically)*

SAXE: *(looking up from paper)* Why, he couldn't take Jackie away from you.

MARY: *(speaks incoherently)* Maybe he could—with all this scandal . . .

SAXE: How do you know he wants to take Jackie? . . . How does the reporter know?

MARY: They must know something . . . how am I going to get out of here?

SAXE: *(trying to soothe her)* Now Mary, be sensible. If you run away now people will believe the worst.

MARY: *(hysterically)* I don't care what people believe . . . I won't lose Jackie. Get me out of here, Saxie . . . I'll take Jackie to Europe . . . quick, we mustn't lose any time . . . see when a plane leaves . . . we'll go to Europe . . .

She hurries out, followed by Saxe talking—

SAXE: *(as he follows her out)* Mary, we should call my lawyer first. I don't believe Lonny would even try such a dirty trick . . . and he couldn't do it anyway . . . *(they are out of the room)*

MARY'S VOICE: But I'm afraid . . .

FADE OUT

82

FADE IN

EXTERIOR STREET—DAY
Medium long shot. Showing foreign street with signs in French or Spanish and foreign atmosphere.

LAP DISSOLVE

EXTERIOR VILLA—DAY
Medium shot—showing small but charming Villa with a wall.

LAP DISSOLVE

EXTERIOR GARDEN—DAY
Full shot—showing portion of garden with gate in wall and part of the Villa with a door leading from it into garden. Mary is digging around plants. She wears a charming sun hat and smart overalls. Bonita comes from Villa followed by a French cook.

EXTERIOR GARDEN—DAY
Medium shot. Mary digs as Bonita and cook enter scene.
BONITA: *(she has a phrase book in her hand)* Miss Evans, this here French cook don't understand her own language. Ah been tellin' her to make rice puddin' with raisins and all she does is bark at me like a dog— oof! oof!
COOK: *(in French)* All I ask is how many eggs Madame, and how many raisins?
MARY: *(laughs)* She is asking you how many eggs, Bonita. Oeuf means egg. *(to cook in French)* Two eggs Therese, and three quarters of a cup of raisins. One pint of milk.
COOK: *(in French)* Merci, Madame. I know how it is made. *(she starts back)*
BONITA: Oof means egg. This here new French language has got me down.
At this minute a French nurse comes dashing through the gate, in a hysteria of excitement.
NURSE: *(in French)* Madame! Madame! Has Jackie arrived yet?

83

MARY: *(in French)* Why no, Therese.

NURSE: *(in French)* A man took him. He said he would bring him home to you. I only went to buy a newspaper and when I returned, the man was playing with Jackie.

BONITA: What is it, Miss Evans?

MARY: Someone has taken Jackie.

NURSE: *(in French)* He said not to be alarmed ... that he was Jackie's papa—

BONITA: *(excitedly)* What's she jabberin', Miss Evans?

MARY: She says Jackie's father has taken him ...

And at this moment Jackie's voice is heard and the garden gate clicks.

JACKIE'S VOICE: We can get in this way—

Everbody turns and sees—

EXTERIOR GARDEN—DAY

Medium shot. Borden and Jackie open the gate and enter. The nurse runs forward and grabs up Jackie in her arms, talking in French.

NURSE: There you are, mon petite. Thank God you are all right. What a fright I have had.

Borden walks over to Mary.

EXTERIOR GARDEN—DAY

Medium close shot.

MARY: *(in French to Nurse)* Take Jackie in the house, Therese.

NURSE: Oui, Madame.

JACKIE: *(calls to Borden)* The frog is over there. *(points to a fountain or wherever)*

BORDEN: Thanks, Jackie. I'll look him up.

EXTERIOR GARDEN—DAY

Medium shot. Nurse with Jackie enters Villa, followed by Bonita.

EXTERIOR GARDEN—DAY

Medium close shot. Mary stands facing Borden.

BORDEN: Hello, Mary.

MARY: How did you find us?

LONNY: *(grinning)* Detectives. I kidnapped Jackie because I knew I could never get in to see you without him.

MARY: What have you come for?

LONNY: *(reaching in his pocket)* Well, among other things, I have an important message for you from Mr. Julius Saxe. *(Mary puts out her hand for it)* No, let me read it to you. *(he reads)* Dear Mary—Just bought a new story. It will make a great comeback for you. You shoot two villains and go to prison for the man you love. Exhibitors are interested. Mama and I send love. JULIUS SAXE

P.S. And you better remarry Lonny Borden. He loves you...he has always loved you...he isn't good enough for you but he'll do anything if you'll take him back. He's really a marvelous young man and he adores you...

MARY: *(suspiciously)* Let me see that letter. *(he shows it to her. She hastily looks at it)* I don't see all that about you.

BORDEN: No—but it's true. And a lot more.

MARY: You didn't go to Hollywood to take Jackie away from me?

BORDEN: Of course not, dear. I went there to help if you needed me.

MARY: Oh, Lonny!

BORDEN: How about having dinner with me tonight?...There's an hotel here with a magnificent main dining room and a fifteen piece orchestra...and orchids...

MARY: *(smiling through tears)* What'll happen if I say no?

BORDEN: You know what happened the last time.

> *He takes her hand and looks down at her without speaking. She looks at him for a long minute, then goes into his arms. He holds her close—no kiss.*

FADE OUT

THE END